AF506166

Japan's "Guest Workers"

Japan's "Guest Workers"

Issues and Public Policies

Haruo Shimada

Translated by Roger Northridge

UNIVERSITY OF TOKYO PRESS

Publication of this book was partially supported by grants from the Japan Foundation and the Suntory Foundation.

ISBN 4-13-047061-2
ISBN 0-86008-498-1

Printed in Japan

Contents

Preface

Japan has a serious foreign worker problem which is likely to play a major role in shaping the nation's future.

The collapse of the 1980s economic "bubble" has plunged the nation into a long, drawn-out recession, and it seems almost as if the labor shortage that was felt so urgently a few years ago had never happened; instead there is now widespread concern over a labor surplus and the possibility of layoffs. Meanwhile, interest in the foreign worker problem, which attracted so much attention when people were worried about the labor shortage, now seems to have abated.

However, Japan's foreign worker problem has by no means been resolved, nor has it in any sense gone away. The population is aging fast, and from now on the size of the younger segments of the population, and therefore of the workforce as a whole, looks set to decline very rapidly. The Japanese people have grown accustomed to affluence, and young people in particular are increasingly reluctant to take jobs that seem hard or demanding. Hence, regardless of the state of the economy, the industries in which such jobs are concentrated face an increasingly serious and recalcitrant local shortage of labor. Once the economy recovers even slightly, serious labor shortages will immediately recur.

In the late 1980s, when the economy was booming and the illegal employment of unskilled foreign workers was escalating, there was a lively debate over how Japan should deal with its foreign worker problem. Some argued that the nation should open its doors and freely accept foreign workers, while others called for a closed-door policy, excluding foreign labor altogether. Today, however, reality has already gone far beyond the parameters of that debate.

The task for Japan today is to squarely face the fact that large numbers of foreign workers and their families are already in the country and have begun to settle on a permanent basis. The main task for the future is to promote a comprehensive policy which as rapidly as possible sets up the conditions that will enable them to work with peace of mind and lead normal lives in Japanese society.

The goal of future policy should be to establish a carefully thought-out institutional structure for accepting foreign workers and to set up a skills training system which ensures that foreigners are not just treated as an easily available source of unskilled labor but are invited to master skills that are of use to them and to the Japanese economy and society. Such a policy should create the institutional and environmental conditions—ranging from medical care, education, and housing to full participation in society—that will enable foreign workers to live in Japan without anxiety.

The future of the Japanese economy and society, the nation's position in the world, and its international reputation will very largely depend on whether or not it adopts such policies and how effectively it is able to implement them. In this sense Japan's response to the foreign worker problem is a litmus test of the kind of nation it seeks to become.

In April 1993, the government issued a Ministry of Justice notification—a very low-key method of announcing a new policy since such notifications rarely receive any public attention—to give its official seal of approval to a new "skills work-training" system for foreign workers. Since this system for the first time officially sanctions the employment of unskilled foreign workers, it should be seen as a major new development in Japan's immigration policy.

People concerned with the issue both in Japan and overseas are now showing strong interest in such policy choices as demonstrating how Japan aims to deals with and ultimately resolve its foreign worker problem.

Several other nations have already attempted to solve similar problems, each in line with its own particular circumstances and experiences, but practically no nation has met with unqualified success. In fact, the foreign worker problem seems to be growing more and more intractable as economic disparities widen, political unrest increases, ethnic and religious disputes erupt, and in many parts of the world increasingly large numbers of people migrate across national borders. Hence international interest has come to focus on Japan and whether, since it is in a position to learn from the experience of the other industrialized nations, its policy choices can somehow establish a definitive method of resolving the issue.

Obviously it will be no easy task to achieve a favorable resolution of such a complex and difficult problem. If Japan continues to react to the foreign worker problem in the same way it has done up to now, it will only exacerbate the damage to society and the economy of which the first signs are already visible, as ever larger numbers of foreign workers come into the country. This does not mean, of course, that Japan either can or should exclude foreign workers totally. Indeed, if it could unconditionally integrate them into Japanese society, the "problem" might well vanish of its own accord. Yet it is probably wishful thinking to imagine such integration to be possible.

The best option that remains to Japan, therefore, is to try and create a more open, but self-reliant, nation. In other words, if it does choose to accept foreign workers, it should work to create a fair and open society that guarantees them exactly the same rights as those it grants its own citizens. But to do this will involve enormous tangible and intangible costs, and necessitate considerable soul-searching by individuals and reform of the society as a whole. To effect such changes in a responsible way will therefore mean building a more efficient economy that no longer needs to rely excessively on foreign labor.

I should like to express my appreciation to the many individuals and institutions whose invaluable assistance made possible the publication of both this English-language book and the Japanese-language version which was published last year by Toyo Keizai Shimposha. Space does not permit me to list all of their names, but I should particularly like to thank the Japan Foundation and the Suntory Foundation for their financial assistance of the translation. Haruo Horioka assisted editorially in various ways. Roger Northridge produced a readable and graceful translation from my drafts. Susan Schmidt of the University of Tokyo Press brought all the pieces together and coordinated the publication of this volume. I will be satisfied if this book provides at least some useful suggestions as to how Japan might best deal with its foreign worker problem in the future.

Mita, September 1993   HARUO SHIMADA

Japan's "Guest Workers"

1

Issues and Policy Proposals

Japan's foreign worker problem is a serious one that will influence the future of the nation to a greater extent than people generally realize.

Japan has become an industrialized nation with a high level of national income, but it faces an aging population and a long-term decline in its workforce, centered on the younger age-groups. Although there is plenty of scope for adapting to these changes in the structure of the workforce by developing labor-saving technology and moving toward a more efficient employment structure, it still seems inevitable that the influx of foreign labor will continue over the long term, owing to the strong demand arising from labor shortages in some sectors, and also to the continuing desire of foreign workers to come to Japan in search of higher earnings.

But how well equipped is Japanese society, either institutionally or psychologically, to accept foreign workers? How rapidly can society prepare for their acceptance, and what institutional form will those preparations take? Is Japan even ready to make the commitment?

If foreign workers continue to enter the country in gradually increasing numbers and provisions are not made for their acceptance, tensions in society, strains in the economy, and possibly outright conflict will result. If the situation slips out of control, the nation will face increasing criticism from the world community and a decline in trust and confidence.

If, on the other hand, Japan had in place a framework for accepting foreign workers, gave them a warm reception in society, and demonstrated that it intended to make a real contribution to the world community by offering them training opportunities, it would command greater trust and respect in the eyes of the world.

But this cannot be achieved without considerable effort and deter-

mination. The nation will have to make deliberate institutional reforms, and the Japanese people will have to change their mind-set
drastically if they are to acquire the wisdom and tolerance to coexist
with people of other cultures. The foreign worker problem, then, is
a crucial test of Japan's ability to reform and to carve out a brighter
future in international society.

Defects of the Current System

Illegal employment is a serious problem that to some degree afflicts all
industrialized economies. In Japan's case, however, the problem is
particularly acute, since illegal workers are a majority of the workforce in many areas.

One reason for this is Japan's legislation relating to foreign workers.
The current Immigration Control and Refugee Recognition Law takes
a strict line, permitting residence to foreign workers with special skills
or knowledge but prohibiting those without such skills or knowhow
from residing in the country for purposes of employment.

While this stance may in itself be justified, there is a widening gap
between the official legal position and the actual state of affairs. Illegal
employment continues to increase, due to the strong demand from
Japanese industry for foreigners prepared to do unskilled work and to
the strong desire of people in other countries to work in Japan where
they know they can earn high wages.

In trying to remain in business, Japanese employers now find themselves caught in a double bind. On the one hand there is a shortage of
Japanese workers willing to do necessary unskilled jobs; yet on the
other hand, while there are any number of foreign workers willing to
do these jobs, employers are unable to employ them openly and pay
them a fair wage, and so are forced to employ them illegally in secret.

Foreign workers are able to enter the country under the sponsorship of brokers, but once in Japan most are forced to work illegally
and treated in effect as criminals. They lack proper protection as
workers, and are more or less compelled to live in hiding. The black
market in foreign labor profits only the brokers and underground
organizations, and is extremely unhealthy. It also arouses the suspicion, in the workers' countries of origin and the world at large, that
Japan is operating a deceptive labor policy, claiming it does not
officially admit foreign workers while continuing to introduce foreign

labor without proper respect for workers' human rights, in response to the demand from Japanese industry.

In addition, the gradually increasing influx of illegal foreign workers will lead to tensions in Japanese society and distortions in the economy. Since illegal workers are relegated to an underground existence because of their illegal status, no one has any grasp of the real situation. Hence there is no guarantee that employers will respect their basic human rights as workers, and this dangerous state of affairs could lead to deteriorating health, the formation of ghettoes, various social problems including crime, and the creation of a permanent underclass in society. Dependence on cheap foreign labor also threatens the working conditions of Japanese marginal workers and could impede efforts to modernize industry.

The Need for a Basic Law on Foreign Workers

Government agencies and other bodies concerned with the issue have made some effort to improve the situation. Policy proposals have been made by government departments, political parties, industry groups, private sector research organizations, labor unions, and many other organizations and opinion leaders. And these have led to some policy changes.

The revised Immigration Law implemented in 1990 makes it easier for foreign workers with specialist skills and knowledge to enter Japan, but denies resident status to those without such skills and knowledge, and institutes tougher penalties for working illegally. At the same time, however, the law allows unskilled workers to enter the country as trainees, while a Ministry of Justice proclamation has made it possible for even small businesses to accept foreign trainees legally. This may have met the demands of industry to some extent, but at the same time it appears to have raised excessive expectations, among small businesses now suffering from a labor shortage, that they will be able to use trainees as a source of labor.

The report issued at the end of 1991 by the Third Administrative Reform Council's Subcommittee on Japan's Role in the World proposed an on-the-job-skill-training (*ginō jisshu*) program, and set out a policy that would essentially permit the use of unskilled foreign workers as a workforce, by allowing trainees to continue to work in the capacity of employees after completing their period of training. Since

Administrative Reform Council reports tend to be strongly reflected in government policy decisions, this proposal normally should have resulted in some legislative action, or at least should have dictated subsequent policy on foreign workers.

After continuing for some time to move in the general direction indicated by the proposal at the practical level, the Ministry of Justice issued an official notification in April 1993 which formally instituted the principles set out in the proposal in the form of a "skills work-training system."

In practice, a small organization called JITCO (Japan International Training Cooperation Organization), which was set up jointly by the government and the private sector, has been accumulating experience in advising and assisting with the reception of trainees; and a number of private organizations have been working in this area under the guidance of JITCO.

A skills training system will be developed on the basis of these practical experiences, and qualified trainees who have completed accredited training programs and wish to work utilizing their new skills will be able to do so.

This system in theory overcomes the contradictions that were defects of the previous training system. In my judgment, the system takes an important step forward in the sense of opening up opportunities for yet-to-be-skilled foreign workers to work in Japan once they have acquired certain basic skills through appropriate training programs. However, I do have some worries about whether the system, as it stands, will achieve the result it hopes to attain.

One problem is that the system itself is difficult for the public to understand, because it has been presented only in the form of obscurely worded announcements from the Ministry of Justice. An announcement which is obscure and difficult to understand even in Japan can have little hope of being visible or understandable overseas, to people who might be interested in coming to Japan to work. A system like this, which is as relevant as immigration laws to the non-Japanese public, should be presented in the more visible form of a law.

Another problem is ensuring that foreign trainees really acquire adequate skills under this system. The process is more than just a legal prescription and definitions. An adequate process of skill acquisition will require a well-organized system that takes into account the many problems that can arise and actually assists participants in achieving their goals.

Developing a Comprehensive Work-and-Learn Program

Allowing unskilled foreign workers to work in Japan is no different in practical terms from granting an amnesty to those who have already penetrated the Japanese labor market as illegal workers and allowing them to work legally. But this will not solve the problem.

One vital prerequisite for a solution is that these workers acquire a certain level of skill through their experience working in Japan. They must be able to lead normal lives in society, learn job skills and techniques, make friends, save a certain amount of their earnings, and return to their home countries with favorable impressions and positive feelings about their experience. But there is no guarantee this can be achieved by enacting a single law. If the various government bodies, organizations, employers, and ordinary people are to help foreign workers integrate in this way, they need guidance and support based on a carefully thought-out policy.

It should not be left just to the government to promote such a policy. The Japanese bureaucracy is very effective at carrying out policies once they are decided but has little capacity for setting out new policies in response to changing circumstances. As has repeatedly been demonstrated in the past, even if one government department does come up with a new policy, reform is eventually rendered impossible by the mutually obstructive behavior of the other departments, each of which is an empire unto itself. What Japan needs more than anything is the political awareness and leadership to overcome these administrative weaknesses and develop a comprehensive policy.

This book advocates the idea of a "work-and-learn program" as the basis of such a comprehensive policy plan. This program, which I have been consistently advocating for the last five years, is explained in greater detail in Part II of this volume, but here let me list its principal features.

First, the program would establish and clearly define "work-and-learn" as a new category of residence status under the Immigration Law. Unskilled foreign workers participating in the program would be granted this status on entering the country, and would acquire skills as they worked. While their main purpose would be training, they would also be doing real work, and would therefore be paid a fair wage and guaranteed their rights as workers.

Second, a placement agency for work-and-learn employment would be set up under the program. This body would be run jointly by the government and the private sector, and be responsible for the acceptance, placement, and support of trainees. Its work would cover many areas: negotiating with the countries of origin over the acceptance of trainees, surveying and analyzing the needs and conditions in Japanese businesses accepting trainees, establishing and revising suitable training methods, regulating the total numbers and distribution of trainees, implementing and providing support for education and training, guiding and counseling trainees, evaluating and testing skills, and maintaining contact with trainees after their return to their own countries. The work would be complex and wide-ranging, and there would be a vast amount of it. With tens or hundreds of thousands of trainees enrolled in the program each year, both central and local governments would be required to earmark a substantial budget and make a major commitment to carry out this work.

The third main feature of the program would be a network of basic education and training centers. Foreigners wanting to work in Japan should acquire in advance the basic skills, such as Japanese language skills, that they will need to live and work in the country. The program would set up basic education and training facilities to help them acquire these skills, both at key locations in their own countries and throughout Japan. A curriculum would have to be developed for use in these facilities, and since it would be desirable for ordinary citizens to take part in the program as Japanese language teachers, a scheme could be devised to facilitate their participation.

Importance of Intermediate Skills Formation

For the work-and-learn program to achieve real results will require above all the involvement and cooperation of both the trainees themselves and the employers participating in the program.

Employers would have to fulfill three basic conditions. They would have to pay trainees an appropriate wage, provide them with suitable accommodation, and, most important, assist them in acquiring intermediate skills—skills which can be acquired in two to five years of training coupled with work experience, but which are sufficiently basic that, on the average work site, trainees can be entrusted to perform them in safety. They are neither the simple, elementary skills of temporary assistants nor the advanced skills of professionals with long years of experience. Intermediate skills are the sort of skills anyone can acquire with a certain amount of study and experience.

Such skills are among the most useful in any industry and type of job. Anyone who has worked in a job for some years would come to possess them, yet in most cases detailed descriptions of these skills and of the training and experience needed to acquire them have not been compiled. An urgent task for policymakers is to study the intermediate skills in a wide range of industries and types of job, set out clear descriptions of these skills, and draft guidelines that can readily be referred to by employers on work sites.

Employers would then be able to assist trainees in the acquisition of intermediate skills in accordance with the guidelines. It would be a condition for employers participating in the work-and-learn program that they provide such assistance, and those who did not comply with this condition would have to be excluded from the program. Some sort of monitoring system would be required to make sure employers did help trainees acquire skills. Monitoring could perhaps be carried out by employers' groups participating in the program.

If large numbers of employers made positive and steady efforts to assist trainees in the acquisition of skills, this would serve as a major foreign aid initiative and enable Japan to offer the world a model program for accepting foreign workers, based on the concept of aid through training, for which there are few precedents anywhere.

Long-term Prospects for Building an Open Nation

The work-and-learn program described above is a medium-term strategy for dealing with the foreign worker problem. It would to some extent resolve the contradiction between the current system and the actual situation, and would provide a channel for the systematic acceptance of unskilled foreign workers seeking employment in Japan, allowing them to work and to acquire skills at the same time.

Such a program is only a medium-term policy, however, since it is based on the assumption that foreign workers are "guests" and will eventually return to their own countries. But in the long term we have to assume a rather different set of circumstances. Gradually some foreign workers and their families will settle down in Japan—indeed there are signs that this is already happening—and eventually they will come to form quite a large social group.

The experience of nations that have admitted foreign workers suggests that this is nearly always what happens. Germany's experience suggests it most strongly. Its situation is relatively similar to that of Japan, in the sense that it is not an immigrant nation, like the United States or Australia, nor was it until recently a colonial power like Britain or France. When Germany admitted large numbers of foreign workers from nearby developing countries, notably Turkey, during its period of rapid economic growth in the 1960s, nobody imagined that they would actually settle down in Germany with its high cost of living. But eventually some of them did remain; they had families, their families grew, and in the end they came to form quite a large community within German society. Prevented by their different culture from being assimilated as ethnic Germans, but at the same time unable to readapt to their countries of origin, they have remained outsiders. Today, Germany is having to make enormous efforts to integrate these people into society, and is incurring huge costs in the process, when it is already reeling under the additional burden of socially and economically integrating the former East Germany.

Japan has already passed the point of no return along the same road. There is no turning back now. At first it will seem that only a tiny number of foreign workers are settling down in the country, but eventually they will be a large subgroup in society. People must come to grips with this reality and strengthen their resolve to ensure that the situation does not develop in a way that would be unfortunate for all concerned.

In doing so they should never lose sight of two points. First, if Japan is to accept foreign workers, it must welcome them as individuals with full human rights and not treat them merely as a source of labor. This means guaranteeing them all the human rights that are enjoyed by Japanese citizens, and all the rights they need to function freely in society as normal citizens. As workers, they must be guaranteed the right to receive proper compensation for accidents at work, medical insurance and unemployment benefits, the right not to be discriminated against either at work or socially, the right to a pension, and the right to vote in local elections. Along with these institutional rights, however, the Japanese people must also adjust psychologically to the idea of real social equality, so that foreigners are not discriminated against in areas outside the legal realm like marriage, where they are entitled to freedom of choice as individuals. If we are going to accept foreigners, we must treat them in a completely open, fair, and equal manner.

Second, there is still a great deal of room for improvement in Japanese employment practices and for greater efficiency in the employment structure. Japan should do all it can to reform its employment system so that it can run its domestic economy as far as possible without relying on foreign labor.

It is easy to hold up the principle of equality, but anyone who claims that such equality can be fully implemented can hardly be living in the real world. Considerable discrimination still exists even in nations made up of immigrants like the United States and Australia. In the former colonial powers, too, however equitable their societies may appear on the surface, deep divisions and prejudices still lurk beneath. It is easy to criticize such discrimination but next to impossible to abolish it. It may be a weakness, or a behavior pattern, inherent in the human condition. The recent ethnic strife in Yugoslavia, for example, clearly demonstrates just how difficult it is to overcome.

Faced with these human failings, the best course of action is surely to increase the efficiency of the domestic workforce and create an employment structure that does not have to rely on foreign labor. Fortunately there is ample scope for such change in the Japanese economic structure, in industry as a whole, and in individual businesses. By doing its best to reform the employment structure, Japan will be in a better position to extend a positive welcome to foreign workers, accord them equal rights, and treat them the same way as Japanese citizens. This will minimize the various social problems that could arise from opening the doors to foreign workers, and is the best way to ensure that the situation develops to our mutual advantage and not to our mutual detriment.

Part I

An Overview of Japan's Foreign Worker Problem

2

The Foreign Workers and Their Problems

Over the last ten years the influx of foreign workers into Japan appears to have accelerated. Since exact data are not available, let us try to make an assessment of their numbers using the available data.

Of some three million foreigners who enter Japan annually, the majority are tourists and other short-stay visitors; only a small proportion enter for the stated purpose of employment. These are Japan's legal foreign workers. But one of the serious problems Japan faces is that there are now large numbers of illegal workers in the country as well.

1. The Present Influx of Foreign Workers

Table 2.1 shows the number of foreign workers entering Japan for the years 1976 to 1989. During this period, the number of people entering the country for employment purposes increased from approximately 20,000 a year to more than 70,000. We can see from the table that the rate of increase accelerated sharply in the mid-1980s.

Table 2.1 also gives a breakdown of foreign workers by category of residence status under the system before revision began in 1990. Categories include "business," "professor," "entertainer," "technical advisor," and "skilled labor." More than half of all foreign workers are classified as entertainers, and entertainment is also the category that has increased most markedly in recent years; the majority of these people are singers and dancers working in red-light districts, most of them women from the Philippines.

The number of foreigners entering the country legally to work in sectors other than the entertainment industry is no more than about 10,000 a year, a negligible amount when set against Japan's total

Table 2.1   Number of Foreign Workers Entering Japan for the First Time

Year	Total Number of First-time Immigrants	Commercial Business (4-1-5)	Professor (4-1-7)	Entertainer (4-1-9)	Technical Advisor (4-1-12)	Skilled Labor (4-1-13)	Residence by Special Permission of Minister of Justice (4-1-16-3) Employment	Foreign Language Teacher	Subtotal
							Purpose of Employment/Residence Status Category (Prior to 1990)		
1976	739,496	9,497	184	10,738	1	307	1,446		22,173
1977	826,156	8,575	197	10,939	2	327	1,716		21,756
1978	835,370	7,845	202	13,132	11	309	1,051		22,550
1979	893,987	7,879	238	18,995	20	336	1,476		28,944
1980	1,087,071	7,244	277	20,580	20	475	1,706		30,302
1981	1,330,720	6,568	274	26,615	11	484	1,923		35,875
1982	1,479,859	7,063	269	23,844	10	550	871	1,027	33,644
1983	1,667,585	6,781	327	25,035	11	408	979	1,041	34,582
1984	1,783,689	6,887	336	32,952	10	511	883	1,196	42,775
1985	1,987,905	6,826	310	34,569	13	498	314	1,464	43,994
1986	1,710,450	6,773	333	44,989	18	552	716	1,355	54,736
1987	1,787,074	6,177	350	59,693	24	465	756	1,718	69,183
1988	1,960,320	6,141	405	71,026	19	480	1,304	2,032	81,407
1989	2,455,776	5,280	449	60,546	13	468	1,688	3,534	71,978

Source: Ministry of Justice, Immigration Bureau, "Annual Immigration Statistics."

Note: Because of changes in the system, the definitions of residence status categories after 1982 differ slightly from those before 1982.

Table 2.2   Number of First-time Immigrants by Residence Status Category

Residence Status	1990	1991	1992
Total	2,927,578	3,237,874	3,251,753
Diplomat/Official Business	22,358	22,318	22,359
Employed			
Professor	591	570	843
Artist	1,202	52	40
Religious Activities	1,958	2,073	2,015
Journalist	410	401	283
Investor/Business Manager	3,807	1,523	1,388
Legal/Accounting Services	42	7	7
Medical Services	73	4	4
Researcher	458	823	860
Instructor	4,092	2,651	2,573
Engineer	1,338	3,166	2,979
Specialist in Humanities/ International Services	2,756	6,416	5,703
Intra-company Transferee	1,540	3,780	4,639
Entertainer	75,091	89,572	84,368
Skilled Labor	1,510	2,381	2,441
Total Employed	94,868	113,599	108,143
Cultural Activities	1,920	3,097	3,538
Temporary Visitor	2,730,793	2,979,547	2,984,805
College Student	9,528	9,620	10,368
Pre-college Student	20,851	20,654	27,367
Trainee	37,566	43,649	43,627
Dependent	10,744	12,739	14,399
Designated Activities	3,935	5,173	5,744
Dependent of Japanese National	13,543	22,820	25,552
Dependent of Permanent Resident	165	260	254
Long-term Resident	8,154	4,398	5,597
Others	155	0	0

Source: Ministry of Justice, Immigration Bureau statistics.

Note: Figures do not include those re-entering or leaving the country on re-entry permits.

labor force of over 65 million. While an increasing number of foreign workers are entering the country, then, only a tiny fraction of them come to Japan as legal members of the industrial workforce. On the face of it, therefore, Japan appears to have clamped down strictly on the admission of foreigners to its industrial workforce. One might even say it has maintained an effective closed-door policy with regard to the introduction of foreign labor.

Table 2.1 gives figures only up to 1989 because a new and substantially revised Immigration Control Law (explained in detail in the next chapter) was implemented on June 1, 1990. The revised law made significant changes to the residence status categories for foreigners entering Japan for employment purposes. Table 2.2 shows the number of immigrants entering the country for work purposes subsequent to 1990, by revised residence status category. We can see from the table that the number of immigrants for employment purposes continued to rise substantially, with 90,000 in 1990, over 110,000 in 1991, and numbers remaining high in 1992, though the rate of increase has fallen off somewhat.

These figures represent foreign workers entering Japan for the first time, but what about those already resident in the country? Table 2.3 shows the number of resident foreign workers by residence status category, as defined by the old immigration law, while Table 2.4 shows the number of residents for each of the revised categories of the new law.

The tables show that, whereas resident professors, foreign language instructors, business people, and skilled workers far outnumber new immigrants in these categories, there are only about one fourth as many residents as new immigrants in the entertainment category. In other words, employment in the entertainment industry tends to be short-term, with a rapid turnover, whereas people engaged in education, research, or ordinary jobs in industry stay for longer periods of time. Nevertheless, the total number of officially employed foreign residents is no more than 80,000, a mere drop in the ocean compared to the total Japanese workforce.

Number of Trainees and Students Rapidly Increasing
There are other types of residence status that allow foreigners effectively to work under certain conditions, while not recognizing them as foreign workers per se. Trainees, pre-college students, and college stu-

Table 2.3   Number of Foreign Workers, by Residence Status Category, under Old Immigration Law

Purpose of Employment/Former Residence Status

Year	Total Number of First-time Immigrants	Commercial Business (4-1-5)	Professor (4-1-7)	Entertainer (4-1-9)	Technical Advisor (4-1-12)	Skilled Labor (4-1-13)	Residence by Special Permission of Minister of Justice (4-1-16-3)		Subtotal
							Employment	Foreign Language Teacher	
1974	749,094	3,494	413	2,035	32	650	(data unavailable)		6,634
1984	840,885	5,943	1,007	7,346	13	1,366	3,004	1,799	20,478
1986	867,237	7,148	1,120	10,357	12	1,502	6,242	4,264	30,645
1988	941,005	7,638	1,322	14,792	22	1,723	7,644	7,257	40,398
1989	984,445	8,071	1,459	15,950	17	1,925	12,468	9,494	49,384

Source: Ministry of Justice, Immigration Bureau.

Notes: (1) Annual figures are those as of December 31.

(2) The 4-1-( ) designations of residence status refer to their respective numbers in Clause 4, Paragraph 1 of the Immigration Law before the revised law was implemented on June 1, 1990.

(3) Because of changes in the system, the definitions of residence status categories after 1987 differ slightly from those before 1987.

Table 2.4 Number of Registered Foreign Residents by Residence Status Category (Purpose of Residence)

Residence Status	1990	1992
Total	1,075,317	1,281,644
Diplomat/Official Business	n.a.	n.a.
Employed		
Professor	1,824	2,575
Artist	560	166
Religious Activities	5,476	5,599
Journalist	382	362
Investor/Business Manager	7,334	5,057
Legal/Accounting Services	76	66
Medical Services	365	198
Researcher	975	1,328
Instructor	7,569	5,841
Engineer	3,398	9,195
Specialist in Humanities/ International Services	14,426	21,863
Intra-company Transferee	1,488	5,135
Entertainer	21,138	22,750
Skilled Labor	2,972	5,352
Total Employed	67,983	85,487
Cultural Activities	1,929	3,317
Temporary Visitor	16,467	33,333
College Student	48,715	56,309
Pre-college Student	35,595	46,644
Trainee	13,249	19,237
Dependent	37,829	44,771
Designated Activities	3,260	4,558
Dependent of Japanese National	130,218	209,269
Dependent of Permanent Resident	14,466	7,864
Long-term Resident	54,359	122,814
Others	2,490	3,701

Source: Ministry of Justice, Immigration Bureau statistics.

Notes: (1) Residence status categories are as defined under the revised Immigration Law.

(2) Total figures for numbers of residents are available only for alternate years; hence no figures are given for 1991. Totals are those as of December 31.

(3) Some categories are not listed, so the sums of the figures for each category do not necessarily correspond to the totals given.

dents fall into this category. They do not possess the relatively high-level skills and knowledge of foreigners admitted to the country for employment purposes; neither are they engaged in any specific type of job. As workers, in fact, they are entirely unskilled, yet they do actually work, at least part of the time, either as trainees whose courses involve work experience or as students doing part-time jobs on the side.[1]

Recent years have seen a rapid increase in the numbers of both residents and new entrants in these categories. The trend is illustrated by Table 2.5, which shows the rapid increase in the number of trainees entering the country. Numbers have more than quadrupled in ten years, from the order of 10,000 in the early 1980s to 43,000 in 1992. During the same period the number of pre-college students attending Japanese language schools increased eleven-fold, from around 2,500 to over 27,000. And the number of college students has more than trebled, from around 3,000 to over 10,000.

Meanwhile, the total number of resident trainees, pre-college students, and college students stands at two to three times the annual number of new entrants. Residents are bound to outnumber new immigrants greatly, since it may take several years to complete a course of study or training.

College or pre-college students are permitted to work part-time for up to four hours a day while studying in Japan, but the system has its problems, and many students are said to use studying as a pretext for working virtually full-time.[2] The trainee system will be discussed in detail in a later chapter, as it has a significant influence on Japan's future foreign worker policy.

The Rapid Increase in Latin American Workers of Japanese Descent
Another notable development is the influx of Latin American workers of Japanese descent. The revised Immigration Control Law of June 1990 permits the children and grandchildren of Japanese nationals who previously emigrated to South America and elsewhere to enter Japan for the purpose of employment, unhampered by the restrictions on residence status that apply to other foreigners. Anyone of Japanese descent, down to the third generation, can now work legally even without specialist skills or knowhow.

Since the system was revised there has been a rapid increase in the number of Latin Americans of Japanese descent entering the country

Table 2.5   Immigration and Residence Statistics for College Students, Pre-college Students, and Trainees

a. Number of First-Time Immigrants

| Year | Study | | Subtotal | Trainee (4-1-6-2) |
	College Student (4-1-6)	Pre-college Student (4-1-16-3)		
1976	2,010	no	2,010	(9,291)
1977	2,199		2,199	(10,641)
1978	2,075	data	2,075	(12,052)
1979	2,141		2,141	(15,124)
1980	2,627	available	2,627	(17,469)
1981	2,892		2,892	(20,237)
1982	3,410	2,556	5,966	9,973
1983	3,912	3,448	7,360	11,929
1984	4,329	4,140	8,469	13,262
1985	4,797	8,942	13,739	13,987
1986	5,419	12,637	18,056	14,388
1987	5,812	13,915	19,727	17,081
1988	6,435	35,107	41,542	23,432
1989	7,777	18,183	25,960	29,489
1990	9,528	20,851	30,379	37,566
1991	9,620	20,654	30,274	43,649
1992	10,368	27,367	37,735	43,627

b. Number of Residents

| Year | Study | | Subtotal | Trainee (4-1-6-2) |
	College Student (4-1-6)	Pre-college Student (4-1-16-3)		
1974	5,712	no data available	(5,712)	no data available
1984	14,172	3,522	17,694	4,270
1986	20,456	15,144	35,600	5,175
1988	29,154	47,827	76,981	8,727
1989	36,839	44,097	80,936	10,817
1990	48,715	35,595	84,310	13,249
1992	56,309	46,644	102,953	19,237

Source: Ministry of Justice, Immigration Bureau survey.

Note: Figures up to 1989 are for residence categories under the old Immigration Law; those for 1990-92 are for categories under the revised law.

Table 2.6   Latin American Workers of Japanese Descent: Numbers and Countries of Origin

a. Number of Workers	
1988	8,450
1989	29,300
1990	76,150
1991	148,700

b. Distribution by Country (as of June 1991)	
All of South America	148,700
Brazil	120,000
Peru	18,000
Argentina	8,500
Bolivia	1,500
Paraguay	700

Source: Ministry of Foreign Affairs estimates.

Note: Figures are approximate. There are an estimated 1.28 million ethnic Japanese in Brazil, 80,000 in Peru, 30,000 in Argentina, 6,000 in Bolivia, and 7,000 in Paraguay.

to work.[3] Table 2.6 shows the annual number of such immigrants since 1988, and their countries of origin for recent years. The table shows that the number of South Americans of Japanese descent coming to Japan to work increased seventeen-fold in a mere three years, from 8,400 in 1988 to 148,000 in 1991.

Untold Numbers of Illegal Workers

We have briefly assessed the number of foreign workers entering Japan for the purposes of legal employment, but these are not the only foreigners actually working in the country. It is well known that several times this number are working illegally.[4]

Although there is no way of knowing exactly how many illegal workers there are, we do have some clues that enable us to make a reasonable guess. One such clue is the annual number of infringements of the Immigration Law. Some of the foreign workers who are found to be engaged in activities their status does not permit started working after entering the country as tourists or to visit relatives;

Table 2.7 Foreigners Apprehended for Violations of Immigration Law, by Type of Offense

Offense	1983	1984	1985	1986	1987	1988	1989	1990	1991	1992
Total	4,768	6,830	7,653	10,373	14,129	17,854	22,626	36,264	35,903	67,824
(1) Illegal immigration	443	513	460	597	542	616	2,349	2,320	1,662	3,459
(2) Illegal landing	59	100	123	124	134	149	258	357	347	573
(3) Activities not covered by residence status	823	357	218	349	372	839	696	751	882	393
(4) Overstaying visa	3,115	5,569	6,592	9,215	12,792	15,970	19,105	32,647	32,820	63,265
(5) (and engaged in activity not permitted by residence status)	(1,516)	(4,426)	(5,411)	(7,782)	(10,935)	(13,475)	(15,912)	(29,133)	(30,405)	(61,768)
(6) Criminal offenses	328	291	260	288	289	280	218	189	192	174
(3) + (5) Illegal workers	2,339	4,783	5,629	8,131	11,307	14,314	16,608	29,884	32,908	62,161
(of which, men)	200	350	687	2,186	4,289	8,929	11,791	24,176	25,350	no data available

Source: Ministry of Justice, Immigration Bureau statistics.

Notes: (1) The following offenses are grounds for deportation: illegal immigration (entering Japan without a valid passport); illegal landing (coming ashore without permission); engaging in activities not permitted under one's current residence status (since June 1, 1990, this has meant receiving income or other remuneration solely from a business not permitted by one's residence status); and remaining in the country illegally after one's legal period of residence has expired.

(2) The number of "illegal workers" is derived from the sum of those found to be engaging in activities not permitted by their status and those who have overstayed their visas as well as engaged in such activities. For 1991, however, the figures for illegal immigrants, illegal entrants, and criminal offenders also include the numbers of those found to have been illegally employed.

others continued to work after their visas expired. The number of people discovered to be working illegally in this way gives us a rough guide to the total number of illegal workers. Table 2.7 shows the annual number of illegal workers discovered since 1983, by type of offense. In 1983, 2,239 foreigners were found to be working illegally, but this figure had risen to over 10,000 in 1987, and to almost 30,000 in 1990.

Nearly twice as many illegal workers were discovered in 1990 as in 1989, but this was due to special circumstances. With the implementation of the revised Immigration Control Law in June 1990, many illegal workers started to fear punishment and turned themselves in, resulting in an exceptional increase in the number of arrests. While the revision of the law played its part, however, increasing numbers of illegal workers are still being apprehended, and the rate of increase has been dramatic in recent years, with fourteen times as many people now being discovered as ten years ago.

Of course the number of people exposed is only a small fraction of the total number of illegal workers in the country. The immigration authorities and the police have neither the capacity nor the personnel to round up more than a very small number of offenders. Nevertheless, it is highly significant that over the last ten years, and particularly in the last few years, the rate of increase in the number of illegal workers exposed has accelerated. This suggests that the iceberg below the surface—the total number of illegal workers in the country—is also swelling at an ever-faster rate.

There is one further clue to the true number of illegal workers in Japan: the number of foreigners overstaying their visas, which can be estimated by correlating immigration with emigration records. The Ministry of Justice's Immigration Bureau has published these estimates on a regular basis since summer 1990, and they are shown in Table 2.8.

The figures show a marked upward trend. Approximately 106,000 foreigners remained in the country illegally as of July 1990, but this had risen to around 160,000 in May 1991, 216,000 in November 1991, close to 280,000 in April 1992, and over 290,000 in November 1992.[5]

Most of those now remaining in the country illegally are from Thailand, Korea, Malaysia, the Philippines, and China. There was a dramatic increase in the number of Iranians prior to May 1992, but

(*text continues on p. 30*)

Table 2.8   Estimated Number of Foreigners Remaining in Japan Illegally, by Country of Origin and Gender

(Unit: persons)

Nationality or Country of Origin	July 1, 1990	May 1, 1991	November 1, 1991	May 1, 1992	November 1, 1992
Total	106,497	159,828	216,399	278,892	292,791
Men	66,871	106,518	145,700	190,996	193,059
Women	39,646	53,310	70,699	87,896	99,732
Thailand	11,523	19,093	32,751	44,354	53,219
Men	4,062	6,767	13,780	20,022	24,463
Women	7,461	12,326	18,971	24,332	28,756
S. Korea	13,876	25,848	30,976	35,687	37,491
Men	8,703	17,977	20,469	22,312	21,406
Women	5,083	7,871	10,507	13,375	16,085
Malaysia	7,550	14,413	25,379	38,529	34,529
Men	5,023	10,099	18,466	27,832	24,150
Women	2,527	4,314	6,913	10,697	10,379
Philippines	23,805	27,228	29,620	31,974	34,296
Men	10,761	12,905	13,850	14,935	15,778
Women	13,044	14,323	15,770	17,039	18,518
Iran	764	10,915	21,719	40,001	32,994
Men	645	10,578	21,114	38,898	32,086
Women	119	337	605	1,103	908

China	10,039	17,535	21,649	25,737	29,091
Men	7,655	13,836	16,624	19,266	21,198
Women	2,384	3,699	5,025	6,471	7,893
Bangladesh	7,195	7,498	7,807	8,103	8,161
Men	7,130	7,429	7,725	8,003	8,047
Women	65	69	82	100	114
Pakistan	7,989	7,864	7,923	8,001	8,056
Men	7,867	7,731	7,786	7,862	7,896
Women	122	133	137	139	160
Taiwan	4,775	5,241	5,897	6,729	7,283
Men	2,080	2,356	2,790	3,427	3,757
Women	2,895	2,885	3,107	3,302	3,526
Peru	242	487	1,017	2,783	6,241
Men	172	339	646	1,904	4,441
Women	70	148	371	879	1,800
Others	18,739	23,706	31,661	36,994	41,430
Men	12,663	16,501	22,450	26,535	29,837
Women	6,076	7,205	9,211	10,459	11,593

Source: Ministry of Justice, Immigration Bureau statistics, released February 1993.

Note: These estimates are based on the immigration and emigration forms submitted by foreigners on entering and leaving the country. But they are subject to numerous discrepancies, so the totals cannot be said to give a true picture of the number of overstayers, and can only be taken as rough estimates.

Table 2.9 Trends in Composition of Illegal Workers, by Nationality

Nationality or Country of Origin	1982	1986	1987	1988	1989	1990	1991	1992
Total	1,889	8,131	11,307	14,314	16,608	29,884	32,908	62,161
	(184)	(2,186)	(4,289)	(8,929)	(11,791)	(24,176)	(25,350)	(47,521)
Malaysia	—	—	18	279	1,865	4,465	4,855	14,303
			(15)	(265)	(1,691)	(3,856)	(3,892)	(11,301)
Iran	—	—	—	—	15	652	7,700	13,982
					(13)	(648)	(7,611)	(13,781)
S. Korea	132	119	208	1,033	3,129	5,534	9,782	13,890
	(35)	(69)	(109)	(769)	(2,209)	(4,417)	(8,283)	(11,204)
Thailand	412	990	1,067	1,388	1,144	1,450	3,249	7,519
	(25)	(164)	(290)	(369)	(369)	(661)	(926)	(2,408)
China								
China				7	39	481	1,162	3,167
				(5)	(26)	(428)	(981)	(2,599)
Taiwan	775	356	494	492	531	639	460	656
	(84)	(161)	(210)	(223)	(275)	(351)	(225)	(374)
Hong Kong				3	18	22	43	144
				(2)	(15)	(20)	(36)	(125)
Philippines	409	6,297	8,027	5,386	3,740	4,042	2,983	3,532
	(13)	(1,500)	(2,253)	(1,688)	(1,289)	(1,593)	(1,079)	(1,466)

Pakistan	7	196	905	2,497	3,170	3,886	793	1,072
	(7)	(196)	(905)	(2,495)	(3,168)	(3,880)	(793)	(1,068)
Indonesia	—	—	—	—	—	—	180	625
							(156)	(571)
Peru	—	—	—	—	—	—	172	580
							(133)	(424)
Sri Lanka	—	—	—	20	90	831	307	451
				(20)	(87)	(821)	(295)	(415)
Bangladesh	—	58	438	2,942	2,277	5,925	293	390
		(58)	(437)	(2,939)	(2,275)	(5,915)	(292)	(387)
Others	154	115	150	267	590	1,957	929	1,850
	(20)	(38)	(70)	(154)	(374)	(1,586)	(648)	(1,398)

Source: Ministry of Justice, Immigration Bureau, "Immigration and Emigration Statistics."

Notes: (1) Figures for 1982 and for 1988–90 represent totals of illegal overstayers engaged in activities + persons engaged in such activities though not overstayers.

(2) Figure in parentheses represent the number of men included in the above totals.

(3) Where no figures are given for a country, they are included elsewhere in the column.

since then numbers have declined sharply, and 1992 saw a slower rate of increase in the total number of foreigners overstaying their visas.

While estimates of the number of foreigners remaining in the country illegally give us an important clue to the total number of foreigners working illegally, clearly even these figures represent no more than the tip of the iceberg. As Table 2.9 shows, the great majority of the nearly 4 million foreigners a year entering the country over the last few years are short-stay visitors whose stated purpose of entry is tourism, business, or visiting relatives, and no one really knows how many of these people, during their short stays, engage in illegal work not permitted by their visas.[6] Neither do we have any clear idea how much illegal work is being done by students over and above the hours their visas permit them to work. Considering the potential for illegal work, then, we must conclude that the real number of illegal workers far exceeds the number of foreigners outstaying their visas.

Illegal Workers Take a Greater Role in Japan's Industrial Workforce
What kind of people are these illegal workers, and what kind of work are they doing?

Table 2.10 shows the sex and nationality of the illegal foreign workers exposed by the immigration authorities over the last few years. We can see that the majority come from Korea, Iran, Malaysia, Thailand, the Philippines, and China. There has been a rapid increase in the number of Koreans, Iranians, and Malaysians discovered to be working illegally, while the number of Philippine nationals is declining. Whereas more women than men were found to be working illegally in the past, one is struck by the rapid rise in the proportion of men apprehended in recent years.

Table 2.10 also shows the type of employment engaged in by the illegal workers exposed during 1991. Almost half of the men were employed in construction work, and about a third in production processes or factory work. Hence the majority of the men were making an important contribution to the industrial workforce. By contrast, only 14% of the women were employed in production processes; nearly half were working as hostesses and 8% as prostitutes. The increasing proportion of male illegal workers tells us that the center of gravity of the demand for illegal labor is shifting away from the entertainment industry and toward key industries like manufacturing and construction.[7] To put this another way, the increasing proportion of

Table 2.10   Illegal Workers by Type of Employment

	Men	
	Number	%
Construction workers	24,208	50.9
Factory workers	13,264	27.9
Laborers	2,820	5.9
Dishwashers	1,054	2.2
Cooks	1,031	2.2
Bartenders	893	1.9
Service workers	765	1.6
Warehouse, transport workers	668	1.4
Others	2,818	5.9
Total	47,521	

	Women	
	Number	%
Hostesses	5,030	34.4
Factory workers	2,549	17.4
Prostitutes	1,606	11.0
Dishwashers	1,333	9.1
Waitresses	1,062	7.3
Cooks	567	3.9
Laborers	502	3.4
Service workers	486	3.3
Others	1,505	10.3
Total	14,640	

Source: Ministry of Justice, "Infringements of Immigration Law in 1992" (May 1993).

Notes: (1) The table shows employment categories for illegal workers apprehended from January to December 1992.

(2) "Laborers" refers to manual workers other than construction workers, electrical workers, and transport workers; in practice, workers in this category are mainly sweepers or garbage collectors.

(3) "Transport workers" are mainly engaged in loading and unloading, packing, and other warehouse work.

Table 2.11   Distribution of Illegal Foreign Workers by Employment Location

Metropolitan Area or Prefecture	Total	Men	Women
	62,161	47,521	14,640
Tokyo	17,870	13,339	4,531
Saitama	6,763	5,778	985
Kanagawa	6,582	5,420	1,162
Chiba	5,726	4,215	1,511
Osaka	4,174	2,935	1,239
Ibaraki	3,659	2,407	1,252
Aichi	3,212	2,620	592
Tochigi	2,017	1,572	445
Gunma	1,825	1,518	307
Nagano	1,193	657	536
Shizuoka	1,141	843	298
Mie	1,104	736	368
Yamanashi	909	711	198
Hyogo	860	771	89
Gifu	568	440	128
Kyoto	381	286	95
Shiga	302	279	23
Nara	249	177	72
Fukushima	231	198	33
Niigata	226	100	126
Others	3,169	2,519	650

Source: Ministry of Justice, "Infringements of Immigration Law in 1992" (May 1993).
Note: The table shows the location by region of the employment of illegal workers apprehended from January to December 1992.

male workers hints that unskilled foreign labor, most of it illegal, is gradually becoming an essential production factor for Japanese industry.[8]

Table 2.11 shows the regions of the country where illegal workers were found to be working. It shows that, while the great majority of both male and female illegal workers were concentrated in the Tokyo area, male workers outside Tokyo were quite widely distributed through regions like Saitama, Kanagawa, Chiba, and Osaka, where manufacturing industry is most active, and were making a major contribution to the country's industrial labor force.[9]

2. Foreign Workers and International Movements of Labor

What lies behind the increasing influx of foreign workers into Japan? How significant are such movements of labor across international borders, and what role do they play?

Foreign Labor Drawn by Strong Domestic Demand

Foreign workers are drawn into Japan principally by the strong domestic demand for foreign labor, which is largely determined by a few main factors. The overall demand for labor is dictated by the growth of Japan's economy. As we have seen, the influx of foreign workers picked up speed in the mid-1980s, reflecting the extraordinary growth of the Japanese economy in the second half of the decade. Under this economic growth, which continued until the beginning of the 1990s, propelled by the expansion that is sometimes called the "bubble economy," there was a marked expansion of the total demand for labor, and the labor market as a whole was faced with a severe shortage. This was manifested in a sharp decline in the unemployment rate, or a rise in the ratio of effective labor demand to effective supply, which was felt particularly acutely in younger strata of the workforce. The large increase in the overall demand for labor inevitably boosted the demand for foreign workers.[10]

A second factor determining the demand for foreign labor is wage levels. If demand grows fast enough to outstrip supply, the change in the balance of supply and demand works to raise wage rates. In other words, higher wage levels are an expression of growth in demand through the price mechanism. The higher wages rise, the greater is the drawing power of demand. In addition to this general rule of the market, however, another factor worked very strongly in Japan in the 1980s—the huge hike in the exchange rate.

In the short space of a year following the Plaza Accord of September 1985, the yen rose approximately 100% against the American dollar, the world's key currency. The huge hike in the dollar exchange rate had the effect of greatly appreciating the yen against the currencies of Japan's neighboring Asian countries, which had been linked to the dollar to greater or lesser degrees, and of many other developing countries as well. This raised enormously the level of the wages foreign workers could expect to earn in Japan, and acted as a strong incentive. The sharp increase in the influx of foreign labor, including illegal workers, since the mid-1980s does in fact closely mirror this change in the exchange rate.

Another determining factor is the nature of the demand for labor. We have seen that illegal foreign workers, in rapidly increasing numbers, are generally employed in construction and factory work, and are coming to play a greater role in the productive workforce, but also that they tend to do unattractive jobs with poor working conditions.

Demand for foreign labor, then, is determined by the total volume of labor demand, by price, and by structural factors. Since the 1980s, and particularly in the second half of the decade, all of these factors have worked synergistically to strengthen demand.[11]

Factors Influencing Foreign Labor Supply

Clearly, there must also be supply-side factors contributing to the influx of foreign labor. One such factor is excess labor in the countries that supply labor to Japan. Most of the illegal foreign workers entering the Japanese labor market come from Thailand, Korea, Malaysia, the Philippines, Iran, China, Bangladesh, and Pakistan. And a high proportion of unskilled foreigners working legally are second- or third-generation Japanese from Brazil and other Latin American countries. Nearly all these countries have certain features in common: an insufficient domestic demand for labor, a certain amount of unemployment or underemployment, and a large excess supply of labor.

Of course, the existence of an excess labor supply depends on a country's state of economic development. It is a widely observed phenomenon that countries send labor abroad while their economies are undeveloped and have an excess supply of domestic labor, then switch to become labor-importing countries as their economies start to develop. Japan itself underwent such a change, and recently Singapore, Taiwan, and Korea have been experiencing the same phenomenon.

A second factor determining the supply of foreign labor is the large income differential between Japan and these workers' countries of origin. There were already large income differences between Japan and the neighboring Asian countries due to their differing stages of eco-

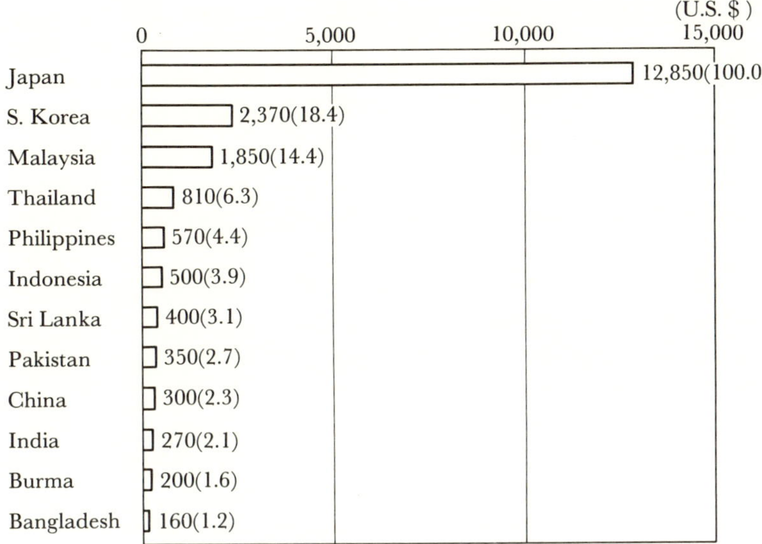

Figure 2.1   Comparative levels of per-capita GNP

Source: 1986 figures from World Bank, "World Tables, 1987."

Note: Figures in brackets are percentages, relative to Japan = 100%.

nomic development, but the huge hike in the yen exchange rate in the wake of the Plaza Accord expanded the income differential still further. Figure 2.1, which compares per-capita GNP subsequent to the Plaza Accord, shows that Japanese incomes are from several times to several tens of times higher than those of neighboring countries. These large income differences act as a strong incentive to people in Asian countries who are contemplating working in Japan.

A third factor is the economic development of the neighboring countries themselves. The foreigners who come to work in Japan do not belong to the lowest social classes in their own countries, in terms of either socio-economic stratum or abilities. They are not just trying their luck in Japan because they cannot get by in their own societies. Instead, they are people with enough initiative to come up with the idea of earning money in Japan, and the ability to raise or borrow the large amounts of money needed for the journey. They have considerable energy and are willing to take risks. They tend to be people with ambitions, who aim to save the money they earn in Japan and use it as capital to carve out new careers and create better lives for themselves after they go back. They have heard about Japan from newspapers and television, by word of mouth or through hearsay; as they develop a familiarity with the Japanese economy and way of life, the incentive to go and work there must grow stronger. As the neighboring Asian countries have developed, the economic distance has grown smaller, exchanges with Japan have deepened, and the country has come to seem closer. And until the economic development of these countries reaches a certain point, the supply pressure from them will probably grow even stronger.[12]

Japan's Immigration Control Law in principle bars people from entering the country for the purpose of employment unless they have special skills or knowhow. With both demand and supply-side factors working strongly to encourage the influx of foreign labor into Japan nonetheless, it is hardly surprising that the rapidly increasing flow of foreign workers should be diverted into illegal employment.

Advantages of the International Movement of Labor

The international movement of labor has a number of basic advantages, particularly in the economic sphere.[13]

First, it can improve the quality of the labor force. Shifting labor from a country with an excess to a country with a shortage both mitigates the excess and alleviates the shortage, achieving a more efficient distribution of labor and other economic resources in both countries. In cases where one country's labor shortage is due to an aging population and a shortage of younger workers, while another country's excess is due to a rapidly growing population and an abundance of young workers, the movement of labor between the two countries serves to improve the quality of both labor forces as well.

A second advantage is that movements of labor activate the labor force. An influx of younger labor from a country with reserves of labor supply to a country with an aging labor force and a shortage of young workers will help activate the labor force of the recipient country. The international movement of labor is also likely to activate the labor force qualitatively. When people from different cultures are thrown together and interact, it tends to stimulate creativity. The United States has traditionally accepted large numbers of immigrants and is still a melting pot for people from different cultures and backgrounds. Though beset by various problems, the U.S. still derives great strength from the creative vitality that results from the coexistence of people from different backgrounds.

Third, movements of labor constitute a form of human-mediated economic aid. For labor-supply countries, workers earning money abroad are a valuable source of foreign exchange, and in many cases the earnings they send home constitute a significant proportion of those countries' service income. In addition, if such workers acquire industrial skills overseas, this becomes a kind of technology transfer to the sender country. So accepting foreign workers can become a powerful form of people-centered economic aid.[14]

A fourth advantage of the transfer of labor is that it helps to relieve unemployment and reduce underemployment in the sender country. Labor-supplying countries often have a comparative excess of domestic labor supply, and sending workers abroad enables them to reduce domestic unemployment or underemployment and to utilize labor and other resources more efficiently.

Fifth, movements of labor contribute to economic development over a wider area. As movements of labor between labor-shortage countries and neighboring labor-surplus countries gradually reduce the differences between them, the labor-surplus countries see a decline in unemployment and underemployment, while the labor-shortage countries see an easing of the bottleneck in labor supply, leading to a more efficient use of economic resources in both countries and promoting economic development in both. In addition, the transfer of income and technology to the sender countries further stimulates development, promotes trade, and furthers the overall economic development of the wider region of which the two countries are a part.[15]

Sixth, movement of labor also could contribute to the national security of the countries concerned by strengthening their economic interdependence. It helps to deepen mutual understanding, makes confrontations and conflicts increasingly disadvantageous, and ultimately promotes security.

Other things being equal, the international movement of labor should confer the many advantages listed above. In the real world, however, the benefits inherent in the movement of labor are seldom fully realized. Instead, movements of workers across borders often seem to cause problems, because so many other factors intervene. The system for moving and accepting foreign labor may not be properly developed, or the recipient country may not be fully capable of adapting to the influx socially, culturally, or politically. Let us now assess the kinds of problems Japan faces in introducing foreign labor under present social conditions, and the adverse effects that may result.

3. Problems Caused by the Influx of Foreign Workers

The single major problem that Japan currently faces in accepting foreign workers is the fact that the great majority are working illegally.

As we have seen, approximately 110,000 foreigners (1992 figures) enter the country legally each year for the purpose of employment, and approximately 85,000 are resident in the country for work purposes. Meanwhile, the immigration authorities each year apprehend about 30,000 foreigners working illegally, and estimate that as many as 290,000 illegal aliens (November 1992 figure) may remain in the country. Clearly the illegal workers caught by the immigration authorities and the police, with their limited means and personnel, represent no more than a fraction of the total number of illegal workers; and while not all of those estimated from immigration and emigration records to have overstayed their visas may actually be working, this figure does not include the unknown segment of the three million immigrants each year who may be doing work not permitted by their status during their legal period of stay. So the figure may be a huge underestimate on this count as well.

The total number of illegal workers must be far in excess of these figures. It is probably several times higher than the number reckoned to have overstayed their visas. But we still have no accurate grasp of the true situation. Taking all this into consideration, one is forced to the reluctant conclusion that a majority of foreign employees in Japan are in fact working illegally.[16]

No Clear Rules
Another major factor that complicates the problem and makes it more difficult to understand is the absence of clear rules governing the acceptance of foreign workers.

This question will be examined in greater detail in the next chapter. Briefly, despite the fact that foreign workers are entering and penetrating the Japanese labor market in many different ways, Japan has only the most rudimentary legislation in place to deal with the problem. Not only are the regulations inadequate; the rules for their implementation are extremely ill-defined.

The fundamental law governing the acceptance of foreign workers into Japan is the Immigration and Emigration Control and Refugee Recognition Law, which allows anyone with specialist skills or knowledge to enter the country for the purpose of employment but strictly bars those without such qualifications from working.

While the law's official position is quite clear, it is being abused in practice, as we have seen, since large numbers of unskilled foreign workers are in fact entering the Japanese labor market. The immigration authorities do of course try to enforce the law, but the problem is that the official stance is extremely unrealistic.

The difficulty stems from the prohibition of admitting foreign workers without specialist skills or knowhow. Demand for foreign labor, not just in Japan but in any country, centers on the types of unskilled work rejected by the domestic workforce. It is only natural, therefore, that demand for unskilled foreign workers should be greater than that for skilled workers, at least in terms of sheer numbers, and the Japanese rules, clear as they are, are quite unrealistic in barring them from entering the country to work.[17]

Of course, unskilled foreigners are not completely prohibited from entering the country. They can enter as trainees or students. Students are allowed to do unskilled work on a part-time basis for up to four hours a day, although only as a concession to help them meet their living expenses. The problem arises with trainees, since the law is by no means clear whether the work they engage in at a certain stage of their training is to be classed as work or not. If it is work, trainees should be paid a fair market wage, and should be guaranteed various basic rights as workers.

The problem, then, is the tremendous gap between Japan's official legal position on the acceptance of foreign workers and the real state of affairs, and the absence, or ambiguity, of regulations that might bridge this gap. In addition to those with specialist skills and knowhow permitted to work legally under the Immigration Law, large numbers of foreign workers are in fact entering the Japanese labor market. As seen from abroad, however, the conditions and qualifications required for immigration seem extremely vague and arbitrary. Hence, while a few unskilled workers are lucky enough to get into the country legally on the strength of their individual connections, the stream of people entering as illegal workers continues undiminished. An unabated influx of foreign workers under these conditions will give rise to all sorts of problems.

Infringements of Human Rights

First, there is the danger of exploitation and infringement of basic human rights. In a situation where so many foreigners are entering the Japanese labor market illegally, there are serious grounds for fear that people will be exploited.

Of course not all illegal workers will be exploited or abused. And limited surveys suggest that working conditions in general are not too bad.[18] When the economy is growing, work conditions improve, and the labor market tends to become a seller's market, with workers switching jobs, being recruited by other firms, and not staying in the same job for long.

However, given that these people are working illegally, we probably would not know about it even if they were being treated unfairly. As the workers themselves cannot register with the authorities, there is no way they can be guaranteed appropriate working conditions, nor can their rights be protected. And numerous instances of unfair treatment have in fact been reported.[19]

A second danger is that the present situation will benefit the underground organizations involved in the employment of illegal aliens. The large number of illegal workers now entering the country will only fuel the activities of the black-market operators who help them get into the country and find jobs. We must not allow these organizations to become any stronger and more entrenched. Not only would that help to propagate their antisocial behavior; it would obstruct any efforts to set up a fair and open system for the acceptance of foreign workers, because such a system would threaten their vested interests.

Delayed Economic Modernization

Third, the continued influx of illegal foreign workers will also obstruct the modernization of Japan's economic structure. Once employers have easy access to cheap foreign labor, it will be easy for labor-intensive industries with relatively poor working conditions to rely on it instead of rationalizing and modernizing their operations by investing in equipment and improving technology. Hence the modernization of labor-intensive industries that have relied on poor working conditions will be delayed.

The history of economic development has been a process in which shortages of labor have led to improved working conditions, which in turn encouraged investment and advances in labor-saving technology that have increased labor productivity and earnings. There is a danger that the simple introduction of cheap foreign labor will interfere with this process of modernization and economic development.

A fourth problem is that it may undermine the working conditions of Japan's own marginal workforce. A huge influx of unskilled labor in the form of illegal foreign workers will threaten the working conditions of domestic marginal workers, who have a complex relationship with foreign workers. Working conditions could easily begin to deteriorate in times of recession in the economy. Marginal workers include the middle-aged and elderly, seasonal workers, migrant workers from rural areas, and part-time workers, whose competitive position is weak. If poor working conditions should become the norm, not only will these people be unable to secure their minimum basic needs but the goal of modernizing the economic structure will be jeopardized.

A Dual Structure in the Economy and Society

A fifth danger is the formation of a dual structure in the labor market. If large numbers of unskilled foreign workers come into the country, and most of them work illegally under poor working conditions, they will gradually come to form a separate stratum at the lower end of the labor market. The formation of such a dual structure not only will delay the modernization of the economy but will have numerous adverse effects on society as well.

Sixth, if the influx of illegal foreign labor continues to increase unchecked, and foreign workers start to form an underclass in society, some of them settling down and forming ghettoes, this could create all manner of social problems.[20]

Most foreign workers have to set aside much of their limited income to send money home, pay back loans, and save, so they inevitably have to pare their living expenses to a bare minimum. But harsh living conditions can pose a threat to their health and nutrition, causing them to fall ill,[21] get into trouble of various kinds, or even become involved in crime. They also may become the objects of discrimination and prejudice. Of particular concern is the possibility that the situation may cause today's children, who will shape the coming generation, to harbor prejudices against other Asians.

A Serious Loss for Japan's Foreign Relations

Seventh, the foreigners coming to work in Japan, while they may be unskilled, do not come from the lowest classes in their own countries. The majority are in their late twenties or early thirties and would normally constitute an extremely valuable labor force in their own countries. Some of them manage to save money in Japan, fulfil their hoped-for objectives, and return home, but many others are discovered and forcibly repatriated, fall ill, or are otherwise frustrated. One can of course say that the workers have only themselves to blame for entering the country illegally, and that is all there is to it, but it is the strong demand from Japanese industry that has drawn them.

While Japanese industry takes on these people at the peak of their productive lives, from their twenties to their early thirties, and enjoys the benefits of their labor, Japan contributes neither to the cost of educating these human resources nor to the cost of supporting them in their old age. It does not guarantee them good working conditions while they are working in Japan, since they are employed illegally; it does not even protect their basic human rights. People in the sender countries have frequently criticized Japan for operating what seems to them a system which, contrary to official Japanese claims, effectively exploits foreign workers.[22]

Eighth, this is a serious loss for Japan's international relations. If Japan continues to convey such a negative impression to the countries from which these workers came, it is bound to damage future relations with them.[23]

Notes

[1] Hiroshi Komai, *The Road to Permanent Residence by Foreign Workers* (Akashi Shoten, 1993), chapter 3.

[2] Komai, op. cit., chapter 1.

[3] Yasuo Kuwahara et al. (Labor Market Research Committee, Subcommittee on the Foreign Worker Problem), "Survey of the Employment Situation among South Americans of Japanese Descent," Tokei Kenkyukai (Statistical Research Association), March 1993. Yasuo Fujisaki, *Migrant Workers of Japanese Descent* (Akashi Shoten, 1993). This work analyzes the situation of

Latin American Japanese workers in some depth, from a historical perspective and from both the South American and Japanese points of view.

[4] Shunichiro Umetani, "The Illegal Foreign Worker Situation," in Tadashi Hanami and Yasuo Kuwahara, *Foreign Workers: Our Neighbors of Tomorrow* (Toyo Keizai Shimposha, 1989), chapter 3. Rey Ventura, *Underground in Japan* (Jonathan Cape, 1992). A remarkably candid account of the experiences of a Filipino working illegally in Japan.

[5] The Ministry of Labor estimates that, as of 1991, there were probably in excess of 480,000 foreigners actually working in Japan, including more than 216,000 who had overstayed their visas. But in actual fact, as explained previously, there are reckoned to be large numbers of illegal workers in addition to those officially identified by the fact that they have overstayed their visas. Report by Special Committee, Ministry of Labor Research Group to Study the Influence of Foreign Workers on the Labor Situation, June 1992.

[6] There were 3,251,753 first-time immigrants during 1992. Ministry of Justice, Immigration Control Statistics.

[7] Komai, *The Road to Permanent Residence by Foreign Workers*. Chapter 2 contains a valuable survey of the actual numbers of illegal workers by industry and type of job, based on observation at work sites.

[8] Tokyo Metropolitan Labor Research Institute, "Employment of Foreign Workers in the City of Tokyo," 1991. People's Finance Corporation, "Employment of Foreign Workers in Medium and Small Businesses," Monthly Report no. 368, December 1991. Medium and Small Business Managers' Accident Compensation Association (KSD), "Report on Foreign Workers: The Situation and Level of Awareness among Medium and Small Business Managers," May 1990.

[9] Kazuaki Tezuka, *Foreign Workers—Part 2* (Nihon Keizai Shimbunsha, 1991), chapter 2.

[10] While some of the demand for foreign labor is due to demand for the specialist abilities of foreign workers, most of it is merely a response to labor shortages. Tokyo Municipal Labor Research Association, "The Employment of Foreign Workers in the City of Tokyo," 1991.

[11] Norikazu Mizuma and Seiichi Kunikata, "The Survival of Medium and Small Businesses in an Age of Internationalization of People: Survey of the Employment of Foreign Workers in Medium and Small Businesses," *People's Finance Corporation Review*, no. 203, February 1992.

[12] Toshio Watanabe, "An Open-door Policy is the Only Response to the Refugee Problem," *Mainichi Shimbun*, September 23, 1989.

[13] Junichi Goto, *The Economics of Foreign Labor: An International Trade Theory Approach* (Toyo Keizai Shimposha, 1990), systematically analyzes the economic consequences of the use of foreign labor, at the points of supply and demand.

[14] At present, since there is no proper system for foreign workers to acquire

skills in Japan, their work experience does not yet serve as a means of technological transfer to their home countries. Kanagawa Prefecture Department of Labor, Labor Administration Section, "Conditions in the Countries Sending Workers to Japan: People's Republic of Bangladesh and Republic of the Philippines," 1991.

[15] Thomas Achakozo, "The Japanese Labor Market: Opening the Doors to Asia," *Nihon Keizai Shimbun*, April 25, 1989.

[16] Yukio Machida, "The Illegal Foreign Worker Situation," *Jurist*, no. 909, June 1988.

[17] The "skills work-training system" approved by a Ministry of Justice notification on April 5, 1993, made it legally possible for trainees who have completed their period of training to use the skills they have acquired in an employment capacity.

[18] Kanto-Area Federation of Lawyers' Associations, *The Employment and Human Rights of Foreign Workers* (Akashi Shoten, 1990).

[19] Aiko Utsumi and Yayori Matsui, *Migrant Workers from Asia* (Akashi Shoten, 1988). Karabao-no-Kai, ed., *"Aren't Foreign Workers Our Comrades? A Report from the Frontline* (Akashi Shoten, 1990). Mainichi Shimbun Tokyo Head Office, City Desk, ed., *Jipangu* (Mainichi Shimbunsha, 1990). Bessatsu Takarajima, no. 106, *The Day Japan Becomes a Multiracial Nation* (JICC Shuppankyoku, 1990), with particular reference to Part I.

[20] While the incidence of various kinds of crime is reported to have increased in step with the escalating influx of foreign workers, this should be seen as reflecting the contradictions between the legal system and economic realities that force people to work illegally. National Police Agency, ed., "Police White Paper," Ministry of Finance Printing Office, 1990.

[21] Ministry of Health and Welfare, Insurance and Medical Service Bureau, Office of Tuberculosis and Infectious Disease Countermeasures, "Survey of TB Registration among Foreigners Resident in Japan," *Data and Outlook*, vol. 1, no. 1, April 1992.

[22] Toshio Watanabe, "Japan is Making the Worst Choice: The Core of the Refugee and Illegal Worker Problem," *Sekai*, January 1991.

[23] Although various opinion polls have shown that most Japanese tend to view the acceptance of foreign workers and their permanent residence in a positive light, proper systems and policies still need to be instituted if this rather abstract demonstration of public goodwill is to be carried through to the level of specific, concrete issues. Information Office, Prime Minister's Secretariat, "Public Opinion Polls Regarding the Immigration and Residence of Foreigners," July 1988; "Public Opinion Polls on the Foreign Worker Problem," November 1990.

3

Policy Responses

There has been a lively debate within the country over the rights and wrongs of accepting foreign workers, and a number of policy proposals have been made by government agencies and other groups. In this chapter, I would like to review the debate on the issue, summarize the main policy proposals that have come out of it, and examine some of the problems inherent in current legislation and policy.

1. The Debate over the Acceptance of Foreign Workers

The Case for Opening the Country to Foreign Labor

As increasing numbers of foreign workers have come into the country, more people are arguing that Japan should abandon its policy of prohibiting foreign labor "in principle," and instead take positive steps to accept foreign workers, moving from being a "labor-closed" country towards becoming a "labor-open" one.

There are a number of grounds for such an argument. First of all, it is to Japan's economic advantage to introduce foreign labor. The rate of increase in the population is gradually falling off, and before long it is expected to start declining. This in itself will aggravate the labor shortage, but at the same time, since the population will be aging as well as declining in numbers, the nation will face an increasing shortage of younger workers. It is argued that, if Japan can unblock this bottleneck in the labor supply by introducing younger workers from neighboring countries which have a relative excess of labor supply and are suffering from underemployment or unemployment, this will not only aid the smooth development of the Japanese economy but will also benefit the labor-supplying countries.[1]

An inevitable consequence of economic development is that while industrialized nations accumulate large amounts of wealth and capital, and generate high incomes, they tend to be relatively short of labor. It is only natural, therefore, that they should compensate for this by introducing labor from abroad, and equally natural that people in developing countries with lower incomes should seize the opportunity to work in industrialized countries where incomes are higher. There is a natural tendency, it is argued, for industrialized countries to open their doors to foreign workers. Indeed, this is one of their roles in the world economy.[2] All over the world, and back through history to the time of the Romans, relatively developed countries have always accepted foreign workers, and there is no reason why industrialized Japan should be an exception to this rule.

A further argument concerns internationalization. With the growing economic interdependence of nations, the increased mobility of commodities, money, people, and information, and closer cultural links between countries, the world is becoming increasingly borderless. Therefore any attempts to set limits on the migration and exchange of labor are anachronistic and run counter to the trend of the times. Japan should look outward, open its labor markets, and allow foreign workers to enter the country freely.[3] This would of course mean an infiltration of Japanese culture at the most fundamental levels, affecting the way people work, their customs and values, and the very nature of society. But proponents of an open labor market feel that Japan would benefit from encouraging change in its society and culture through the introduction of disparate elements.[4]

The Case for Closing the Country to Foreign Labor

Arguments for opening Japan's labor market have been countered by equally strong arguments for a more careful—even negative—approach to the introduction of foreign workers in view of the confusion, negative effects, and social costs such a policy might engender. While some argue for a more comprehensive ban than others, such arguments basically call for a closing of the country to foreign labor.[5] And there are strong grounds for advocating such a policy.

First, the indiscriminate acceptance of foreign workers could be a recipe for social chaos. If Japan throws open the doors to foreign workers before passing appropriate legislation or putting in place the institutional and social systems needed to accommodate them, there is no guarantee they will not be discriminated against and exploited, or that their human rights will not be infringed. Local communities will face problems in supplying housing and education, and there could be an increase in the crime rate.

Opening the country to foreign labor could also have an adverse effect on the economy. Under present conditions, it could well benefit those businesses and industries suffering from a labor shortage, but it would only be a stopgap solution to the problem and makes little sense as a long-term policy for the economy as a whole. Simply depending on foreign labor in this way would retard the rationalization and modernization of labor-intensive industries with their poor working conditions and, in the long term, damage the competitiveness of Japanese industry. The large-scale introduction of unskilled foreign workers prepared to work for relatively low wages would also inhibit and delay the improvement of working conditions for Japan's own seasonal workers and its already disadvantaged marginal workforce. In addition, unskilled foreign workers would tend to form an underclass, encouraging the creation of a two-tiered labor market which would hinder modernization and advances in economic efficiency.[6]

Introducing foreign labor might help to alleviate the immediate labor shortage, but it would eventually entail significant social costs as well. Obviously the immediate costs of wages, welfare, education, and training would be covered by the work that foreigners contributed. But accident compensation and health care for these workers and education for their children would have to be provided if they settled down in Japan, and local communities would have to set up the systems needed to accommodate them into society. In all likelihood, therefore, the total economic and social cost burden incurred through the introduction of foreign labor would outweigh the benefits it conferred.[7] We can gain some idea of the complexity and seriousness of the problem Japan would face from looking at the difficult problems and enormous social costs now faced by Germany in its attempt to integrate the large numbers of *Gastarbeiter* it introduced beginning in the 1960s.[8]

Finally, there is the question of maintaining the cultural integrity of Japanese society. A massive influx of foreign workers could transform not only the economy but many other aspects of the Japanese social order, cultural traditions, and lifestyle. Some critics have argued that such changes could damage the cultural integrity of Japanese society, and might have a profoundly destabilizing effect.

The Case for Accepting the Inevitable

Both the arguments for opening and closing the country have their own basic logic, and can help us understand the various aspects of the issue. But the situation has now developed to a point where these arguments have become largely academic. As foreign workers continue to enter the country and become part of Japanese society, people have gradually come to acknowledge the seriousness of the situation, and the debate has shifted toward the more realistic questions of how to get things moving in the right direction and how best to limit the damage.[9] This debate has focused on three main points.

First, there is the question of how to protect the human rights of foreign workers. As we saw in Chapter 2, the most serious aspect of the problem is that the majority of foreigners working in Japan today are illegally employed. The law prohibits unskilled foreign workers from entering the country for the purpose of employment. Yet we have a situation where large numbers of foreigners are entering the country on various pretexts and engaging in unskilled labor: there is a strong demand for unskilled manual labor to be met, and the workers themselves are strongly motivated by the prospect of high earnings.

Due to their illegal status, these workers do not register with the authorities, and there is no way of accurately assessing what is going on. Although not all of them may be working under unfair conditions or being exploited, there is still no way of protecting workers in the black labor market if they should be treated unjustly or find themselves in a situation where their rights are being infringed.

Furthermore, some of these workers, while they are technically still illegal immigrants, are gradually settling down in Japan, marrying and having children or bringing their families to join them. They are slowly assuming a presence in society outside the confines of the workplace. As this process continues, it is creating problems with potentially serious repercussions, in health care, in education, and in integrating foreigners into local communities.

As the situation has developed, attention has come to focus on how to protect the rights of foreign workers and how to resolve these various social problems.[10]

Second, there is the question of cooperating to create job opportunities in the labor-sending countries themselves. One reason for the increasing numbers of illegal foreign workers in the Japanese job market is the demand for unskilled labor from Japanese employers. But another factor is the supply pressure: while Japan's high incomes and high wages are a strong incentive for foreign workers, they also face a dearth of good employment opportunities at home.

Although they come to Japan in the hope of high earnings, there are also considerable risks involved. In their own countries, the exodus of young workers has an adverse affect on family life and many other undesirable consequences, including the hollowing out of the labor force. Obviously it would be much better if there were good employment opportunities in their home countries and local communities to begin with.

Hence, many have argued, the role of industrialized countries like Japan should be not so much to provide training and employment for foreign workers in Japan as to create job opportunities for them at home, through investment and aid.[11]

There is much to be said for this argument, and Japan should be doing all it can to create jobs in the developing countries. Basically, however, these countries themselves should be centering their development efforts on the creation of job opportunities. Other countries may contribute through investment and aid, but their role must necessarily be a limited one.

Finally, people are calling for the implementation of a careful and systematic policy for the acceptance of foreign labor. As we have seen, many of the complex problems Japan faces today are due to the enormous disparity between the official legal position and the actual state of affairs.

If Japan is to resolve the problems that are arising out of this disparity and still uphold the principle of the law, it will be necessary to make a number of realistic policy adjustments and create some well-designed systems to coordinate the employment of foreign workers.[12]

Opinion leaders, government planners, and others concerned with the issue have come up with many constructive proposals for a realistic resolution of the problem. In the next section, we will examine some of these proposals in detail.

2. Government, Political Party, and Private Sector Policy Initiatives

Over the last few years, the political parties, government ministries and agencies concerned with the foreign worker problem, employers' groups, labor unions, and research organizations have published a number of reports examining the situation of foreign workers, advocating systems and methods for dealing with them, and making a number of new policy proposals. An enormous amount of data on the problem has also accumulated.

The following list includes only the proposals, reports, and materials in my possession. Unfortunately I do not have the space to summarize the content of all the reports, but the discussion that follows the list is based on them.

Political Parties

Liberal Democratic Party Political Affairs Research Committee, Judicial Affairs Section, Subcommittee on Immigration Policy Issues, (Chair, Yoshikazu Ota), "Interim Report on the Immigration and Residence Problems of Foreign Workers," April 1988.

Liberal Democratic Party Political Affairs Research Committee, Labor Affairs Section, Subcommittee to Investigate the Foreign Worker Problem, "How to Respond to the Foreign Worker Problem (Interim Summary)," May 1988.

Liberal Democratic Party Political Affairs Research Committee, Foreign Affairs Section, Subcommittee to Investigate the Acceptance of Foreign Workers (Chair, Yoshiko Otaka), "Interim Report on Problems of Accepting Foreign Workers," April 1988.

Liberal Democratic Party Political Affairs Research Committee, Special Committee on the Foreign Worker Problem, "The Foreign Worker Problem," May 1988.

Policy Commission, Socialist Party of Japan, Special Committee on the Foreign Worker Problem, (Chair, Takanobu Nagai), "Basic Stance of the Socialist Party on Foreign Workers: Five Principles in Dealing with the Foreign Worker Problem," January 1989.

Komei Party, "Proposal for Internationalization at the Local Level," January 1989.

Democratic Socialist Party, "Proposal for a Small Business Recruitment Policy," February 1990.

Government Bodies

Working Group on the Foreign Worker Problem, Ministry of Labor (Chair, Kazuo Koike), "Report by Working Group on the Foreign Worker Problem," March 1988.

International Economy Section, Economic Council, "Report by International Economy Section," Economic Planning Agency, April 1988.

General Policy Section, National Council on Quality-of-Life, "Internationalization of the People's Lives," Economic Planning Agency, April 1988.

Immigration Control Association, "Interim Report, Committee to Investigate the Foreign Worker Immigration Problem" (Summary), May 1988.

Round-Table Discussion to Investigate the Foreign Worker Problem, Ministry of Labor, "Responses to the Foreign Worker Problem," December 1988.

Ministry of Foreign Affairs, "Draft Plan for a Skills Training Program" (tentative title), March 1989.

Economic Planning Agency, Working Group on the Influence of International Movements of Labor on the Domestic Labor Market, (Chair, Haruo Shimada), "Foreign Workers and Socio-Economic Policy," April 1989.

Economic Planning Agency, Working Group on the Influence of International Movements of Labor on the Domestic Labor Market, (Chair, Haruo Shimada), "Foreign Workers and Socio-Economic Policy," April 1989.

General Affairs Section, Industrial Structure Council, "The Future of Japan's Industrial Activity and Industrial Policy under Globalization," Ministry of International Trade and Industry, May 1989.

Working Group on the International Situation, (Chair, Kiichi Saeki, Cabinet Research Office), "The Emergence of the Foreign Worker Problem, and Countermeasures," November 1989.

Round-Table Discussion on Industrial Labor Problems, Ministry of International Trade and Industry, "Response to the Foreign Worker Problem," May 1990.

Working Group on Construction Industry Labor Problems, "Report by Working Group on Construction Industry Labor Problems," Ministry of Labor, June 1990.

National Police Agency, "Police White Paper: The Rapid Increase in Foreign Workers and the Police Response," August 1990.

Ministry of Labor, Working Group on the Influence of Foreign Workers on Labor Issues (Chair, Koichiro Yamaguchi), "Study of the Influence of Foreign Workers on Labor Issues," March 1991.

Special Conference on the Influence of Foreign Workers on Labor Issues (Chair, Koichiro Yamaguchi), "Report," June 1992.

Employers' Groups, Labor Unions, and Other Private Sector Organizations

Committee on International Problems, Kansai Committee for Economic Development, "Towards Internationalization on the Human Level: Promoting Employment of Foreigners," December 1987.

Association of Business Executives, "Future Policy on the Employment of Foreigners: The Systematic Acceptance of Foreign Labor through a 'Work and Learn Program,'" March 1989.

Committee on Employment Problems, Kansai Association of Business Executives, "Promoting Wider Employment of Foreigners: Towards an Open, Multicultural Society," March 1989.

Japan Confederation of Labor Unions, "Demands and Proposals for Policies and Systems (1990–91)"; "Promotion of Measures to Deal with Foreign Workers," 1989.

Tokyo Chamber of Commerce and Industry, "Call for a Labor Policy for the Future," July 1989.

Association of Business Executives, Committee for a Japan Amenable to Foreigners, "Towards Coexistence with Foreigners: Establishing Ideas and Steadily Implementing Specific Policies," July 1989.

Council of the Japan Construction Industry Workers' Union, "Internationalization of the Construction Industry," July 1989.

Tokyo Chamber of Commerce and Industry, "Proposal for the Establishment of a Skills Formation System for Foreign Workers," December 1989.

Japan Federation of Employers' Associations, "Report by Labor Problems Research Group," January 1990.

Japan Food Services Association, "Catering Industry Proposals for the Employment of Foreigners," May 1990.

National Conference on Society and the Economy, "The Labor Shortage and the Foreign Worker Problem," June 1990.

Rengō (Labor Confederation) Institute for Life Development Research, "Towards the Creation of a Human-Centered Socioeconomic System," October 1990.

Research and Survey Institutions
National Institute for Research and Advancement, "Study of the Acceptance of and Coexistence with Foreign Workers" (NIRA Study Series), April 1990.

Small Business Employers' Accident Compensation Association, "The Foreign Worker Problem: Situation and Awareness among Small Business Employers—Report on Foreign Workers" (*KSD News*), May 1990.

National Institute for Research and Advancement, "Study of a System for the Social Acceptance of Foreign Workers" (NIRA Study Series), June 1990.

Information Office, Prime Minister's Secretariat, Prime Minister's Office, "Public Opinion Poll on the Foreign Worker Problem," November 1990.

Kanagawa Prefecture Fact-finding Commission on the Asian Labor Situation (Chair, Kazuaki Tezuka), "The Situation in the Countries Sending Foreign Workers: Bangladesh and the Philippines," February 1991.

Japan Labor Research Organization, "Policy Issues Relating to the Foreign Worker Problem: A Critical Study of Policies in the Main

Countries Accepting Foreign Workers" (Research Report no. 5), March 1991.

Tokyo Metropolitan Labor Research Association, "Employment Situation of Foreign Workers in Tokyo," March 1991.

Employment and Unemployment Research Group, Employment Promotion Association (Chair, Akira Takanashi), "Study of Employment Problems and Changes in the Economic and Industrial Structure: A Response to the Foreign Worker Problem," March 1991.

Labor Market Research Committee (Nakamura Takafusa et al.), "The Labor Market and Changes in the Economic Structure—The Acceptance of Foreign Workers and the Japanese Labor Market," Statistical Research Association, August 1991.

International Training Cooperation Organization, "Annual Data on Overseas Trainees, 1992," October 1992.

Subcommittee on the Foreign Worker Problem, Labor Market Research Committee (Chair, Yasuo Kuwahara), "Fact-finding Study of the Employment Situation of Japanese South Americans," Statistical Research Association, March 1993.

These proposals and reports offer constructive suggestions on what specific responses government agencies, employers, and others should make to the now ineluctable foreign worker problem. These proposals have provided policymakers with many suggestions for policy choices and system design, and have had a certain amount of influence. Let us now examine in more detail the proposals and reports which are thought to have been particularly influential in shaping subsequent policy.

Employment Permit System
The "Report on the Foreign Worker Problem," published in March 1988 by a Ministry of Labor working group chaired by Professor Kazuo Koike, looked at the problem in a wholly new light and advocated an employment permit system, which would have the following three features:[13]
(1) Employment permits would be issued to employers. Any business anticipating employing foreigners would be required to obtain permission.

(2) Employment permission would be granted to employers who intended to employ foreigners who possessed high-level skills or knowledge—specialists, technicians, managerial workers, qualified professionals, and foreign-language instructors—or who had completed skills-training programs or graduated from a Japanese university, in cases where it was deemed that work experience would either improve their qualifications or contribute to the development of their home countries. The scope of the system would be interpreted as broadly as possible under the laws in force at the time. Refugees and foreigners with permanent residence would be exempt from the system, and there would be no restrictions on their employment.

(3) When employers took on foreign workers they would have to obtain employment permits in advance. Employers would be eligible for such permits only on the conditions that their businesses were financially sound, they could provide acceptable working conditions for their employees, they were capable of fulfilling their obligations as employers, and they did not violate the law in any way.

Compiled at a time when the steady influx of foreign workers into the Japanese labor market was beginning to raise difficult social, economic, and legal questions, the report can be appreciated as a positive attempt to improve or resolve these problems within the framework of the Immigration Law in force at the time, before it was revised in 1990.

The main object of the proposal seems to have been to gain an accurate grasp of the employment situation among foreigners resident in Japan, through their employers, by granting employment permits to employers rather than work permits to workers, as is done in most other countries. The number of illegally employed foreigners is rapidly escalating, due to the gap between the formal position of the Immigration Law and the actual state of affairs. Hence the first step toward improving things is to set up a system under which the real numbers of foreign workers can be accurately assessed. The employment system can be seen as an effective means to this end; it has the additional advantage of serving as a check on employers' compliance with the law.

In the end, however, the Labor Ministry proposal was not implemented, and indeed has not been studied thereafter in any great depth.[14] One reason was the strong opposition from the Ministry of Justice, which opposed it on several grounds: (1) Requiring employers to obtain official permission before drawing up a private contract of employment only in the case of foreigners would breach the principle of equality with Japanese nationals, contravene the international code of human rights, and run counter to the spirit of the Japanese Constitution. (2) It might have a discriminatory effect on the business activities of the more than 700,000 long-term Korean residents in Japan. (3) The permit system was designed to combat the problem of illegal employment, yet the foreigners required to obtain permits would already be legally employed, so it would do nothing to solve the problem. (4) Foreigners would resent it as a further burden of red tape in addition to that for the immigration and residence permissions they had already obtained.

Undeniably, the proposal for an employment permit system did present some legal and administrative problems. Nevertheless it is essential to obtain the participation and cooperation of employers in some form or other. Only then can the illegal workers who have gone underground come out into the open under conditions where they can be provided with proper protection. I think, therefore, that the concept of using employers to control the situation continues to merit serious study.

Work-and-Learn Program
In March 1989, the Keizai Dōyūkai (Association of Business Executives) published a report entitled "Future Policy on the Employment of Foreigners: The Systematic Acceptance of Foreign Labor through a 'Work-and-Learn Program,'" compiled by a Committee on Future Employment (chair, Masahiro Sekimoto, then president of Nippon Electric Corporation). As chair of the committee's working group, I was involved in the design of the proposal for a work-and-learn program and in the drafting of the report. Since we came up with the initial proposal, I have become increasingly convinced that for some time to come Japan is going to need some such well-designed, systematic program, implemented on a wide scale, if it is to resolve or alleviate its foreign worker problem. And since the publication of our report, the government has step by step moved closer to implementing the concept of work-and-learn employment that we advocated. Let us take a look at the report's main proposals.

(1) Foreigners with high-level knowledge or skills should be positively encouraged to enter the country, but the easy and irresponsible introduction of foreign labor should be avoided.

(2) The report proposes, as a medium-term policy, a "work-and-learn program" which would make a positive contribution to the international community in the sense of investment in human resources. The work-and-learn program would accept foreign workers in a systematic way and educate and train them in job skills, basically through on-the-job-training in private industry. Workers would be paid the same wages as Japanese for the work that they did. They would be returned home after they had completed a certain period of training, thus avoiding the social friction and problems that might arise if they were to stay on in Japan.

(3) Funds from Japan's ODA budget would be used to set up "basic training centers" in major cities in the sender countries as well as within Japan, at which trainees would be educated in the Japanese language and basic knowledge about the country.

(4) A "coordinating organization," to be run jointly by the government and the private sector, would be set up to coordinate the needs of the sender countries and employers in Japan and to monitor implementation of the program.

(5) In addition, the report stresses the need for progress in clamping down on illegal employment, developing adequate job opportunities within Japan, and effecting the changes in popular perceptions and the institutional reforms that will lead to a more open society.

These are the main points covered by the report. The work-and-learn proposal, which is also a principal theme of this book, is discussed in greater detail in Chapter 4 below.

Conditions for Integration

The Economic Planning Agency's "Foreign Workers and Socio-Economic Policy," edited by its General Planning Office in April 1989, was one of the earliest attempts to state the problem; it presented, at a relatively early stage in the debate, a number of scenarios, including the concept of "integration."

The report was commissioned by the Economic Planning Agency from a private think-tank, which set up a working group, chaired by the author, to "survey the influence of international labor force movements on the domestic labor market." The group studied the potential impact of accepting foreign workers from all angles, taking its cue from the five-year economic plan "Coexisting with the World," drawn up in 1988, which calls for a "prompt and careful examination" of the foreign worker situation "with due regard to its various repercussions."

This report was the first to talk about "integration," and while it was commissioned by a government agency at a relatively early stage, when the foreign worker influx was just beginning to become an issue in Japan, it attracted attention because it was understood to be advocating a policy of indiscriminate acceptance. This was not actually the report's intended message, however. It merely studies, from a long-term perspective and, literally, "from multiple angles," the consequences that might be expected to arise from accepting foreign workers.

The report classifies possible systems for accepting foreign workers into four basic patterns: "laissez-faire," "seclusion," "migrant worker control," and "integration." A laissez-faire system would maintain the apparatus of the current immigration law, which accepts foreign workers with special skills and denies entry to those without such skills, and would make no attempt to implement any additional policies. It concludes that the pursuit of current policies unchanged would do little to prevent the emergence of illegal employment on a massive scale.

A "seclusive" system would take the strongest possible steps to halt the influx of illegal workers. But not only would this entail enormous direct costs; it would have a major impact on industrial output and on international relations.

A "migrant worker control" system would accept unskilled foreign workers subject to very strict controls. Such a system could be expected to go some way toward answering the needs of Japanese industry, which is short of labor for unskilled jobs, and to improve on the current situation, in which the problem of illegal workers has largely been abandoned as a lost cause. However, controlling immigration in this way would also involve significant costs, and many practical problems would arise in deciding what methods of control to employ and what standards of judgment to apply.

An "integration" system demands that both the government and the private sector make strenuous efforts to ensure that the foreigners Japan has accepted can be absorbed into society and coexist with it. Such a policy could be expected to have significant repercussions on Japanese society and the economy, and whether it succeeded or not, the report concludes, would depend very largely on the receptivity of Japanese society to extraneous elements and on its capacity to coexist with heterogeneous cultures.

Which of these four patterns Japan adopts will be dictated not just by economic considerations but very largely by other conditions in society and by Japan's international situation. Looking at all aspects of the situation, it would seem that a "migrant worker control" policy is the most realistic option for the time being, but that Japan ought to consider the "integration" approach for the long term.

Actually implementing such a policy would require a great deal of preparatory groundwork, however. Integrating foreign workers would require the implementation of a wide range of measures not just in areas directly related to employment but also in social security, school education, community participation, and language. Japan would have to institute various new public-sector initiatives and work to modify social customs. The workers themselves and the countries they come from would also have to make strong efforts to integrate on their own account.

Skills Formation System for Foreign Workers

In December 1989, the Tokyo Chamber of Commerce issued a very specific "Proposal for the Establishment of a Skills Formation System for Foreign Workers."

The proposal advocates that Japan "set up a 'skills formation system for foreign workers' that will coordinate the acceptance of foreign workers, and accept, under fixed conditions as to numbers, length of stay, working conditions, and training methods, foreign workers whose object is to acquire a certain level of skills, techniques, or knowledge while working." The main points of the proposal are as follows.

(1) *Conditions for Acceptance*

Candidates should be able to speak basic Japanese and have the desire, after acquiring a certain level of skill or knowledge through their work experience, either to seek employment as skilled workers on their return to their home countries or to set up independent businesses. In principle candidates should be single. They would sign an employment contract with the firm employing them, and be subject to all labor-related laws and enrolled in labor and health insurance systems. But part of their insurance contributions would be set aside for a special fund to assist in repatriation. Trainees enrolled in the system would stay for a maximum period of two years in principle. There would be a ceiling on the number of trainees accepted, and this would be adjusted annually with reference to the employment situation.

(2) *Bilateral Agreements with the Sender Countries*

The government would draw up bilateral agreements with countries sending workers, stipulating conditions of acceptance, including workers' qualifications, conditions of employment, period of stay, type of job, and numbers; sponsorship by the sender countries; methods of operating the basic training facilities set up in the sender countries; and the method of repatriation of trainees who have completed their periods of training.

(3) *Acceptance Organizations*

A centrally placed acceptance organization would be responsible for basic planning, information processing, consultation with sender country organizations, and administration of the repatriation fund. Separate local organizations would draft regional acceptance plans, screen applicants, mediate with employers, and conduct all business related to the repatriation of foreign workers. Both central and local organizations would hold conferences and give help and advice with regard to plans and policies.

(4) *Obligations of Businesses Accepting Trainees*

Businesses accepting trainees would draw up plans covering job-type, numbers, period of employment, working conditions, and career plans, and submit applications to the acceptance organizations. Firms accepting foreign workers would have to conform to all relevant labor legislation, guarantee fair pay and protection of human rights, and make efforts to ensure that foreign workers had the opportunity to acquire skills and qualifications. They would also in principle bear the various costs involved in accepting trainees.

(5) *A Skills Training and Skills Accreditation System*

Under the proposed system, candidates accepted for employment would undergo a physical examination and receive prior basic training in the sender country. Basic Training Centers would be set up for this purpose in the sender countries, using ODA funds. Businesses accepting foreign workers would receive grant aid support for the job training they offered. A skills testing and accreditation system would be introduced and made widely accessible. Consideration would be given to granting work visas, under the immigration law, to trainees who had passed such accreditation tests up to a certain level during their period of stay and who wished to find employment where they could use those skills.

(6) *Assistance with Repatriation*

A special fund would be set up to assist in the smooth repatriation of trainees. To ensure the availability of employment opportunities for workers returning home, Japanese companies in the sender countries would be asked to employ them on a priority basis, while local acceptance organizations would provide advice on employment and starting businesses.

(7) *Preventing Illegal Employment*

To prevent illegal employment, the acceptance organizations set up under the proposed system would grant permission and supervise employment for foreigners whose residence status entitled them to work, such as college students, pre-college students, and spouses of Japanese citizens.

3. Policy Developments

Revision of the Immigration Control Law

The most significant development in Japan's policy on foreign workers in recent years was the implementation of the revised Immigration Control Law in June 1990. The Partial Amendment of the Immigration Control and Refugee Recognition Law (generally abridged to "Revised Immigration Law") was passed by the 116th session of the Diet in December 1989, and came into force on June 1, 1990.

While the Immigration Law has undergone a number of minor revisions since it was first enacted in 1956, the 1989 amendment can properly be described as epochal in its scope.[15] Of course strong pressure for amendment of the law came from public concern over the foreign worker problem, which escalated to serious proportions during the late 1980s.[16] One reason, as we have already seen, was the rapid increase in the number of illegal workers; but from a wider perspective, the problem was exacerbated by the world trend toward internationalization, globalization of business activity, and increasing movements of people across national borders.[17]

Broadly, the Revised Immigration Law has three main features.[18] First, with the object of simplifying immigration procedures for highly qualified foreigners with specialist skills or knowledge, the new law reclassifies the various categories of residence status, making them easier to understand and extending their scope.

Second, the revised law reaffirms the strict ban on immigration for the purpose of employment by foreigners without a residence status permitting them to work. This is backed by penalties, which were not prescribed by the old law.

Finally, the new law clarifies the standards for immigration screening, and simplifies the red tape involved. In short, then, the Revised Immigration Law responds to calls for internationalization by making it easier for qualified foreign workers to enter the country, but maintains the ban on workers without specialist skills or knowledge, and takes a tougher stance on admitting unskilled workers.

Although it is somewhat detailed, let us now look at the list of immigration status categories defined by the new law. Table 3.1 is a comprehensive listing of the categories.

The new classification permits employment under 16 categories of residence status, to which is added a seventeenth category, "specific activities," under which employment may or may not be permitted, depending on the nature of the activities permitted to that individual. These categories do not include those permanently domiciled in Japan—either permanent residents and their dependents or refugees—who are permitted to engage in any type of activity without restriction. If we also include college students and pre-college students, who are basically prohibited from employment but who are allowed to work part-time for a certain number of hours a week, the total number of categories permitting employment comes to 19.

Some of the new categories are almost identical to the old categories they replace, while others are redefined or wholly new. The provenance of each of the categories is indicated by a ○ or △ in the table. Categories marked ○ are newly established, while those marked △ have been partially redefined. Unmarked categories are virtually identical to their predecessors. We find, then, that while the revised law introduces ten new residence categories, most of these are categories

(*text continued on p. 67*)

Table 3.1   Activities Permitted by Category of Residence Status

Section 1. Residence statuses permitting foreign nationals to engage in specific activities in Japan

1. Residence Statuses Permitting Employment

(1) Statuses under which immigration is not subject to a Ministry of Justice ordinance

Diplomat	(1) Diplomatic and consular officials, and their dependents
	(2) Persons accorded by treaties or international custom the same privileges or exemption as diplomatic envoys (e.g. foreign heads of state, heads of cabinets or national assemblies, UN secretary-general and heads of UN organizations) and their dependents
Official	Public servants employed by foreign governments or international bodies, employees of foreign diplomatic and consular offices in Japan, and their dependents
Professor	Foreigners employed as professors, assistant professors, or assistants at universities, institutions corresponding to universities, or colleges of higher education
△ Artist	Composers, songwriters, painters, sculptors, photographers, and other artists who derive income from artistic pursuits
Religious Activities	Persons sent to Japan by a foreign religious organization to engage in missionary or religious activities
△ Journalist	Journalists engaged in news-gathering or other journalistic activities in Japan, based on a contract with a foreign newspaper company, news agency, broadcasting company, newsreel company, or other news medium. Specifically, newspaper and magazine reporters, documentary writers, chief editors, editors, news cameramen, TV and radio announcers, including freelancers

(2) Statuses under which immigration is subject to a Ministry of Justice ordinance

Investor/Business Manager	Foreigners conducting investment or business, or engaged in the management of such a business, where the business complies with certain criteria as to size, salary, and past record

Table 3.1　(continued)

○	Legal/Accounting Services	Foreigners holding legitimate Japanese qualifications in the field of law or accountancy, as a lawyer, copyist, real estate surveyor, solicitor in foreign law, CPA or foreign-certified accountant, tax accountant, social insurance advisor, patent attorney, or administrative scrivener
○	Medical Services	Foreigners holding legitimate Japanese qualifications in a medical-related profession, as a doctor, dentist, pharmacist, district nurse, midwife, nurse, practical nurse, dental hygienist, radiotherapist, physical therapist, occupational therapist, optician, clinical technician, or artificial limb fitter
○	Researcher	Foreigners engaged in experimental, survey, or research work based on a contract with the government, a local public body, or special corporation, and foreigners engaged in experimental, survey, or research work based on a contract with an organization other than the above, subject to certain criteria with regard to career and salary
○	Instructor	Foreigners engaged in educational activities at primary, junior high, or high schools, specialist or other types of school. Includes not only persons engaged as teachers at primary, junior high, and high schools and possessing legitimate Japanese teacher's licenses, but also persons engaged in foreign language education at foreign language schools, subject to certain conditions
△	Engineer	Foreigners engaged in work requiring knowledge or techniques in the fields of science, engineering, or the natural sciences subject to certain conditions with regard to career and salary
○	Specialist in Humanities/ International Activities	(1) Foreigners engaged in work requiring knowledge in the humanities—such as law or economics—subject to certain conditions with regard to career and remuneration (2) Foreigners engaged in work utilizing cultural knowledge or sensibilities unique to foreigners, such as interpreters, translators, copywriters, fashion designers, interior designers, also persons engaged in sales, overseas business, information services, inter-

Table 3.1 (continued)

		national finance, design, or public relations and advertising, subject to certain conditions with regard to career and remuneration
○	Intra-company Transferee	Foreigners transferring from a Japanese subsidiary or branch office abroad to its head office in Japan, or from a head office overseas to a branch office in Japan, and engaged in activities covered by "technician," "humanities," or "international activities" status, subject to certain conditions with regard to career and salary
△	Entertainer	(1) Foreigners engaged in theatrical, entertainment, singing, dance, or musical performance activities, subject to certain conditions with regard to career, remuneration, and type of entertainment (2) Foreigners engaged in artistic activities such as television program or film production or photographic modelling, subject to certain conditions with regard to remuneration
△	Skilled Labor	Foreigners engaged in work which requires specialist skills in particular fields in Japanese industry (foreign cooking, production of foreign foodstuffs, specialist foreign building skills, civil engineering skills, gemstone, precious metal or leather processing), subject to certain conditions with regard to career and remuneration

2. Residence Statuses Not Permitting Employment
(1) Statuses under which immigration is not subject to a Ministry of Justice ordinance

○	Cultural Activities	Foreigners engaged in non-remunerative study or artistic activities in Japan, and persons receiving individual instruction from specialists, or conducting specialist research into, Japanese culture or arts (e.g. ikebana, tea ceremony, judo)
	Temporary Visitor	Foreigners visiting Japan for a short period for the purposes of tourism, recuperation, sports, visiting relatives, friends, or acquaintances, visiting the sick, attending ceremonies, amateur participation in events and contests, commercial visits for market research, business meetings, negotiations, contract-signing, or

Table 4.1   (continued)

	after-service of imported machinery, study/observation visits to factories or trade fairs, participation in short courses or presentations, academic research, research and development, religious visits or pilgrimages, or goodwill visits to sister cities, schools, etc.

(2) Statuses under which immigration is subject to a Ministry of Justice ordinance

College Student	Foreigners receiving education at a university or other institute of higher education, subject to certain conditions regarding ability to meet living expenses; includes persons receiving a fixed number of hours of tuition as auditors or research students, or receiving education in a special subject at a specialist college, subject to certain conditions regarding Japanese language ability, etc.
○ Pre-college Student	Foreigners studying at a high school, Japanese language or other type of school, subject to certain conditions regarding ability to meet living expenses
△ Trainee	Foreigners engaged in acquiring skills, techniques or knowledge (not only industrial skills and techniques but also training in administrative skills at local government institutions, and training in office skills) at institutions accepting trainees which satisfy certain conditions as to their ability to provide training, and provided the skill does not consist merely in the repetition of the same action
Dependent	Dependents of persons with residence status from "professor" to "cultural activities" above, and of persons with "visiting student" status

(3) Residence statuses under which employment may be permitted on an individual basis. (Immigration not subject to a Ministry of Justice ordinance)

Designated Activities	Foreigners entering Japan as domestic helpers privately employed by embasssy or consular officials, etc., persons entering Japan under the working holiday system (which is based on bilateral agreements with other countries, allowing young people to work as a means of supplementing their travelling expenses, to increase their opportunities to learn about other cul-

Table 3.1   (continued)

___

> tures and lifestyles), and foreigners employed as amateur sports players by Japanese firms

Section 2. Residence statuses placing no restrictions on activities

___

Permanent Resident	Persons granted permission to reside permanently in Japan (excludes first-time immigrants)
Dependent of Japanese National	Dependents of Japanese citizens, children born as Japanese citizens or specially adopted as Japanese citizens (as defined by Civil Law no. 817, clause 2)
○ Dependent of Permanent Resident	Dependents of permanent residents, permanent residents by agreement, or persons from the Korean peninsula or Taiwan who have resided in Japan since before World War II
Children of Persons Who Have Renounced Japanese Nationality	Children of persons who have renounced their Japanese nationality under the terms of a peace agreement with Japan, who were born in Japan and have lived continuously in Japan (excludes first-time immigrants)
○ Long-term Resident	Refugees as defined by refugee treaties, permanently domiciled Indonesian refugees, persons of Japanese parentage, and permanently domiciled persons having Japanese grandparents

___

Note: The categories of residence status defined by the Immigration Law represent the basic legislative framework for residence by foreigners in Japan. For some categories, however, the law also requires prospective immigrants to conform to certain ordinances laid down by the Ministry of Justice, stipulating additional criteria for the granting of immigration permission, with reference to the potential influence on Japanese industry and on society, and other factors.

that were previously rather loosely or vaguely defined, which have now been redefined more clearly and concretely. They are not in fact wholly new categories.

Most of the activities lumped together by the old law under the designation 4-1-16-3 (residence specially permitted by the Minister of Justice) have been reallocated to specific professional categories. Clarifying these categories of residence status has made immigration standards much clearer. Ministerial ordinances defining immigration screening criteria have made the system clearer than under the old law, while the introduction of a residence status certificate system has abbreviated and speeded up the immigration screening process.

Interest Focuses on Trainees

The new immigration law was a substantial improvement on the old one. It redefined and reorganized the categories of immigration status, reviewed and improved the screening process, and instituted stiffer penalties. Yet it still failed to give clear answers to some of the questions that most concerned the public, and that particularly concerned industry.

The revised law clearly defines the categories of residence status permitting employment to foreign workers with specialist skills or knowledge, and spells out the rules more clearly. It also reaffirms the principle of prohibiting employment to workers without such abilities. Nevertheless, the new law does not do much either to reassure industry or to legitimize the status of unskilled workers seeking employment in Japan, since people who are at present unskilled but capable of becoming more skilled in the future through education and training or work experience—those I have referred to in this book as "to be skilled"—are still regarded by the new law as "trainees" or "pre-college students."

If the government is really committed to the position of admitting workers with specialist skills or knowledge but closing the door on those seeking employment but lacking such skills, then it contradicts its avowed policy by allowing "language students"—who have no such qualifications—to work part-time, and letting trainees do "practical training," i.e., work.

If, on the other hand, the government were to accept the premise that unskilled workers could become more skilled if they were allowed to build up some work experience, it would have to redefine the position of the law with regard to workers who have no special skills.

The term "trainee" sounds fine in principle, but how many employers are really offering trainees any "training," in the sense ostensibly intended by the immigration authorities? How can private-sector companies be expected to take on the additional work of training these people unless they are paid to do so? If they really went by the book, making trainees attend lectures for more than one third of the time and giving them "work experience" for the remaining two thirds, yet not allowing them to do any real "work," they simply could not make ends meet. Clearly, if they did not make trainees work, the costs involved in "training" would leave them substantially in the red.

Of course even private companies do sometimes engage in altruistic activities. Some are seriously interested in skills training, and willing to bear the costs because they want to contribute to society by voluntarily providing educational aid. It can of course be argued that only employers with this level of commitment should be allowed to take on trainees in the first place, but this would exclude nearly all firms from taking part in training programs, and even those allowed to participate would probably still find it difficult to run courses as anything but loss-making ventures.

One could also argue that, while businesses offering to train foreign workers could not expect to turn a profit in the short term, their educational efforts would eventually reward them. While such an attitude is to be welcomed, however, it is hardly prevalent enough to encourage really broad-based participation in a training program. Most small businesses simply do not have the leeway to take such a long-term view.

Why then does industry show such a high level of interest in "trainees"? Indeed it is more than just interest, since, as we saw in the previous chapter, there has been an enormous increase in the number of trainees accepted by private industry over the last few years.

What really interests employers, of course, is that, while gaining "practical work experience," unskilled trainees are in fact doing relatively low-grade manual work. Calculating the value of this work, they figure that a small outlay in training costs is not such a bad investment. No doubt some employers train foreign workers purely as an act of charity, as official policy would have them do, and meet the costs out of their own pockets, but such cases are probably quite rare. For most firms accepting trainees, the benefit consists in the work that they do, coupled with the fact that employing trainees enables them to avoid having to pay workers a market wage, since the law obliges them to pay trainees only a small "training allowance."

To this extent, the "trainee" system has always been something of a charade. It is shot through with contradictions: trainees do real work in the guise of "work experience," yet it is not counted as work; they are not paid proper wages for the work that they do; and furthermore, despite the fact that they are working, they are deprived of the guarantees—in the form of accident and health insurance—that, as workers, they naturally are entitled to.

As I will argue at greater length in the next and subsequent chapters, so long as trainees are engaged in real work, their status as workers should be formally acknowledged, and they should be granted full workers' rights. And if trainees are to be considered workers, yet if both workers and employers are to be motivated to raise the level of trainees' skills, the correct policy can only be to institute a systematic training program along the lines of the work-and-learn program advocated in this book. This matter will be discussed in greater detail at a later stage.

On August 17, 1990, shortly after the Revised Immigration Law came into force, the Ministry of Justice issued two important proclamations, numbers 246 and 247, which "stipulate special criteria governing residence status for trainees" and which have enabled trainees to be accepted by a broader range of organizations. Whereas trainees could previously only be accepted by public bodies which ran trainee programs, like the Japan International Cooperation Agency (JICA) or the Labor Ministry's Central Human Resources Development Council, or by businesses planning to expand overseas and participating in government or local authority-run programs, these proclamations broke new ground in opening the way for large numbers of ordinary small and medium-sized businesses to accept trainees as well.

The proclamations mean that smaller businesses are now able to accept foreign trainees provided they formally enlist in a program run by chambers of commerce, local merchants' associations, or small business organizations. The only condition is that such training programs must be funded and otherwise supported by the government or a local municipal authority.

Previously, since firms could accept only one trainee for every twenty regular employees, small businesses with fewer than twenty employees were effectively barred from participating. The new proclamations, however, permit any firm with fewer than fifty employees to take on up to three trainees. Hence, in theory at least, even a firm with only three employees is now in a position to accept foreign trainees.

Following the proclamations, the Japan Chamber of Commerce

issued a guidebook for firms wanting to accept trainees, and set about educating and instructing chambers of commerce and local business associations throughout the country. Needless to say, small and medium-sized businesses all over the country expressed enormous interest in accepting trainees.[19]

The law continued to cling resolutely to the distinction between "training" and "work," yet small businesses, suffering as they were from a severe labor shortage, were extremely keen to take on trainees, either because they misunderstood the law or because they saw through its facade.

Proposal for a "Skills Training System"
In December 1991 the subcommittee on "Japan's Role in the World" of the Third Administrative Reform Council (chair, Kazuo Inamori) recommended as part of its second report the establishment of a "skills training system."

The main points of the proposal are as follows:
(1) The skills training system would enable trainees to acquire skills while working. To guarantee the effective acquisition of skills, trainees' levels of proficiency would be tested after they had completed a certain period of training. Trainees demonstrating a given level of competence would then be permitted to gain practical experience within an employment relationship.

(2) An appropriate limit would be set on the number of trainees accepted, and they would stay for a period not exceeding two years. Trainees would in principle be restricted to certain types of jobs, and a minimum period of training would be required, though this could be shortened for trainees who already had a good working knowledge of Japanese. After completion of the initial training period, trainees' skills proficiency would be tested, and those who achieved a certain standard would be permitted to embark on a period of practical skills training, during which the usual labor and social security laws would apply and the trainees would be compensated at a uniform rate.

(3) Restrictions would be placed on the accompaniment of trainees by their families, and on changes in the type of job once training had commenced.

(4) Responsibility for repatriating trainees would rest with the employer.

(5) An acceptance organization would be responsible for the supervision of conditions in training courses, testing of skills, consultation with the sender countries, basic education (including Japanese language training) prior to the commencement of training, and the provision of support for small and medium-sized businesses accepting trainees.

These, in brief, are the main proposals of the Administrative Reform Council report. Since the Council was set up with the intention that its recommendations would insofar as possible be reflected in administrative policy, through the drafting of legislation or other means, the report has obviously had a significant influence in determining the course of subsequent government policy on foreign workers.

While the report to some extent adheres to the official line with regard to "training," the principal aim of the proposal is to give unskilled foreign workers practical work experience in the form of "skills training" after they have completed an initial training period. The report does not go so far as to use the word "worker," but it does talk about an "employment relationship" during the skills training period, when "the labor and social security laws would apply," and this can only mean that trainees would effectively be treated as workers. The proposal also allows for some flexibility in the study content of the initial training period, subject to the individual trainee's Japanese language ability and general preparedness, so if trainees had some basic abilities and a working knowledge of Japanese, the study element in the training could probably be cut back to a minimum. In short, the report has significantly eroded the official stance on "training" that the Immigration Law has upheld for so long, and taken a major step toward allowing the introduction of foreign workers primarily as a source of labor.

Japan International Training Cooperation Organization (JITCO)
In October 1991, around the time that the Third Administrative Reform Council's second report was being compiled, an organization with the aim of supporting the acceptance of foreign trainees by the private sector (chair, Akio Morita) was set up under the joint auspices of the Ministries of Labor, International Trade and Industry, Justice, and Foreign Affairs. Subsequently the Ministry of Construction joined the body as well.

The organization is quite modest, with basic capital funding of only about ¥1 billion. It receives an annual government grant of a little less than ¥400 million, and raises the rest of its running expenses from membership fees. But the organization's brief is extremely wide-ranging. It conducts prior surveys and negotiations with the sender countries, and offers member businesses a consultation and information service. Then, at the stage when businesses are preparing to accept trainees, it dispenses advice on training programs, gives guidance on job-training facilities, checks immigration and residence documents, and helps with the paperwork for comprehensive insurance. Once training has actually commenced, it helps with the use of training facilities and provides teaching materials, training instructors, and knowhow for skills testing.

One of the most important services JITCO provides is information on, and help with the paperwork for, comprehensive insurance policies for foreign trainees. Since trainees are not workers, they cannot qualify for the usual forms of workers' insurance. So JITCO enlisted Japanese insurance companies to put together a special policy for trainees. JITCO also develops teaching materials, provides educational and training services, and maintains contact with the authorities in the sender countries and with other trainee organizations.

Under the present law governing the acceptance of trainees, all these various tasks have to be done, and an organization the size of JITCO is hard pressed to cope with the workload. Of course if the government passed a basic law on the acceptance of unskilled foreign workers, and trainees came to be acknowledged as workers, they would be eligible for ordinary labor insurance and there would be no need to arrange special insurance for them. But in any case, to deal effectively with all this ancillary work probably requires the establishment of a very much larger support organization.[20]

JITCO still has only a small number of member firms. If small and medium-sized companies nationwide are to contribute to the acquisition of skills by unskilled foreign workers, they will require a much more closely coordinated service network coupled directly to their needs.[21]

Ministry of Justice Proclamation on Skills Training
On April 5, 1993, a Ministry of Justice notification announced "guidelines on immigration control for a skills work-training system." The

announcement came after consultations within the Ministry of Justice and with other ministries and agencies, with reference to the experience of JITCO and the above-mentioned report by the Third Administrative Reform Council.

The proclamation lists the main points of the skills work-training system as follows:

(1) *Eligibility for Skills Training*

The object of the skills training system is to cooperate in education that will contribute to economic development, through the transfer to the developing countries of more practical skills, techniques, and knowledge (below, "skills").

Participation in the system will be open to persons seeking practical skills training, who are already engaged in training, and have been granted "trainee" residence status under the Immigration Law. Acceptance will be conditional on the fact that, after returning to their home countries, trainees plan to engage in work which necessitates use of the skills they acquired in Japan. Participants will be expected to achieve a level of proficiency in line with the aims of the skills training system. They must demonstrate an intention to acquire skills of a practical nature.

(2) *Testing Skills Proficiency*

To take part in the skills training system, candidates must be certified by a training facility in Japan as having reached a certain level of proficiency. Skills accreditation will be based on the proficiency tests conducted by JITCO.

(3) *Institutions Offering Training*

Institutions offering training will draw up contracts with trainees and remunerate them at the same rate as Japanese employees. When trainees are to continue training in the same skills, they will remain at the same institution. The institution will secure accommodation facilities for trainees and take steps to guarantee their repatriation by, for example, setting aside funds for travel expenses.

(4) *Length of Stay*

The period of practical training will generally be up to 1.5 times the length of the initial training period, but such that the total period of training does not exceed two years.

(5) *Changes in Trainees' Residence Status*

Candidates for training will apply for their status to be changed from "trainee" to "specific activities." Candidates should, as a rule, apply to JITCO to have their skills proficiency evaluated by 3 months before the completion of their current training period.

The April 5 announcement gave concrete shape to the recommendations of the Third Administrative Reform Council report, and set out specific rules for the treatment of trainees under the law.

Unskilled foreign workers, after undergoing a few months of training in Japan as trainees, and provided they have been certified as having reached a certain level of proficiency, can now apply to have their residence status changed to that of "skills trainee" under the new skills training system. If their application is accepted, they can then continue to train at the same firm or institution as workers, this time under an employment contract which will guarantee them the same level of wages as Japanese workers doing the same jobs. The new system enables trainees to stay in Japan for up to two years, including the initial period of study-training and the subsequent period of practical training. The institution offering training, i.e., the employer, will have to provide suitable accommodation, and set up a system to guarantee payment of trainees' return travel expenses when they complete their period of employment.

This "skills training system" is very close to the "work-and-learn program" that I have been advocating for the last five years, and is also very similar to the "skills formation system" envisaged by the Tokyo Chamber of Commerce and Industry, which we looked at earlier. The inauguration of the new system can be said to have resolved, theoretically at least, the problems inherent in the Immigration Law and, more particularly, the welter of contradictions in the training system.

As the system is implemented, attention is likely to focus on two questions: first, whether it will serve to prevent any further increase in the number of illegal workers who have already entered the Japanese labor market in such large numbers; and second, whether it will really enable trainees to acquire appropriate skills, techniques, and knowledge.

4. An Evaluation of Government Policy and the Remaining Agenda

We have reviewed policy development since the revision of the Immigration Law; I would like, finally, to examine the state of Japan's policy on foreign workers today, and point to some problems that still remain.

Legislation and Outstanding Problems

The government deserves credit for many aspects of the policy it has developed. The Revised Immigration Law's clearer classification of residence status categories for foreigners with specialist skills, the improvements in the immigration screening process, and the stricter penalties for illegal employment were all legislative improvements whose time had come.

The government also deserves praise for its April 5, 1993, Ministry of Justice notification, which established a "skills work-training system" along the lines advocated by the interim report of the Third Administrative Reform Council's committee.

As I have repeatedly stated, foreign trainees were previously consigned to a sort of "grey area," since they neither had specialist skills or knowledge nor were totally unskilled. Consequently a huge gulf opened up between the official legal position on the one hand, and the real situation and trainees' expectations of employment on the other. Their status remained fraught with contradictions. The April 5 announcement for the first time officially permits trainees who have completed a certain amount of training and demonstrated a degree of competence to engage in real work. It can be said to have resolved the flagrant contradiction in the law whereby trainees, although they were doing real work, were denied their natural rights as workers.

These policy developments and legislative reforms are to be welcomed, but much remains to be done before we can say with any certainty that they will produce the hoped-for results.

One problem is that the legal position on the treatment of unskilled foreign workers is still not clearly defined. It is true that the new skills training system will enable unskilled foreign workers to learn skills and have their rights as workers formally guaranteed. But how well is the system understood by the many prospective candidates throughout the world? Although governments in the sender countries have been informed of the system's existence, and have at least nominally been supplied with information about it, trainees still know practically nothing about what they must do to take part. Have they been given any specific information as to what qualifications they need, or how to prepare for admission?

Another question is whether or not the skills training system will really help unskilled foreign workers to acquire appropriate skills. While the system is theoretically up and running, the question remains whether the institutional and policy framework is sufficiently solid for it to do the work it is intended to.

The Need for a Basic Law and a Comprehensive Policy
Solving the first of these problems will require the enactment of a basic law governing the treatment of foreign workers, which will set out the legal position clearly and systematically.

At present, while the Immigration Law prescribes the basic rules on immigration, many specific and important legal issues related to training are, as we have seen, covered only by a few stopgap directives in the form of Ministry of Justice proclamations. The rules take a form that is very difficult for outsiders to comprehend. Even Japanese employers have difficulty understanding what qualifications trainees require, or what papers they have to submit, just by reading the relevant laws and regulations, and frequently have to resort to government offices for help in interpreting the law as it applies to specific cases. Would-be trainees from abroad must surely have an even harder time working out what standards and qualifications are required.

These basic rules should be set out clearly and in a form that is easily comprehensible to candidates anywhere in the world, like the conditions stipulated by the immigration laws. Their legal basis should not be hidden away in Ministry of Justice proclamations which ordinary people are not in a position to know about. Standards and requirements must be stated in the law in a way that is clearly and easily understandable by anyone who cares to look.

I strongly endorse the aims of the skills work-training system, which will enable unskilled foreign workers to acquire skills in an employment relationship, with their rights as workers guaranteed. But for the system to become an integral part of Japan's foreign worker policy, it needs to be clearly demarcated so that trainees are given a separate residence status under the Immigration Law, appropriate to the new system and separate from the previous "training" status.

The system needs comprehensive and systematic rules governing labor relations and social security, the various rights and obligations of trainees in society, and their human rights in general. In addition, the organization responsible for screening trainees, supervising and evaluating their training, conducting skills proficiency tests, and managing and operating the system should be given a clear legal status and a proper institutional base that enables it to conduct these activities systematically on a large scale. To clarify regulations and standards, some form of legislation, such as a basic law, is required that sets out such an overall institutional framework.

Resolving the second problem, meanwhile, requires a comprehensive body of policy and an organization capable of effectively implementing the skills training system in such a way that it achieves its stated objectives.

The basic objective of the system is to help unskilled foreign workers acquire appropriate skills that will be of use to both themselves and their countries. What can be done to ensure that this objective is actually attained?

If the system is to ensure that trainees acquire skills effectively, its content must be very clearly defined, and the organizational and policy measures required for its implementation must be very carefully designed. Standards of evaluation must be clearly set out, and effective measures taken to implement them. Policy on training must be designed and promoted in such a way that the workers themselves are strongly motivated to acquire skills, while employers consider it a rational choice to invest energy in helping them to do so.

I have been proposing the concept of a practical training system, or work-and-learn program, for some time. The recent developments in Japan's foreign worker policy that we have surveyed in this chapter appear to be moving step by step in this direction. For these new policy developments really to have an effect, however, the government needs to draft and promote an even more thoroughgoing and institutionalized system and body of policy. In Chapters 4, 5, and 6, therefore, I will describe in some detail a plan for a work-and-learn program, to serve as a reference for the development of future policy.

Notes

[1] Taichi Sakaiya, "If We Accept Foreign Workers," *Nihon Keizai Shimbun*, July 2, 1989, morning edition.

[2] Hiroshi Kurosawa, "Japan in the World: Liberalizing People Is the

Quickest Way to Become an International Nation," *Kokusai Jinryu*, March 1989.

[3] Yasuaki Onuma, "Defects in the Argument for Introducing Foreign Workers," *Chuo Koron*, February 1988.

[4] Yoshimi Ishikawa, "The Open-Door Argument Shows No Concern for People," *Voice*, February 1988.

[5] Kanji Nishio, *Recommendation for a Closed-Door Labor Policy* (Kobunsha 1989).

[6] Kazuo Koike, "Caution in Opening the Nation to People," *Voice*, May 1989. Kazuo Koike, "Blind Spot in the Argument for Accepting Foreign Workers," *Shukan Toyo Keizai*, June 11, 1988, issue.

[7] Kazuaki Tezuka, "Stop and Think before Introducing Foreign Workers," *Chuo Koron*, February 1988.

[8] Kanji Nishio, "The Tragic Error of Internationalizing People: Learning from the Mistakes of West Germany," *Seiron*, March 1988.

[9] Yuji Koido, ed., "Foreign Workers: Policies and Issues," Tax and Accountancy Association, 1990. This publication presents the policy views of government representatives from the Ministries of Justice, Labor, and International Trade and Industry, along with those of labor and administration specialists.

[10] Hiroshi Komai, *How to View Foreign Workers* (Akashi Shoten, 1990), chapter 4.

[11] Goro Ono, "Division of Labor with the Asian Countries Better Than Accepting Foreign Workers," *Bulletin of the Japan Economic Research Center*, October 1, 1991, issue.

[12] Junichi Goto, *Foreign Workers and the Japanese Economy: Some Recommendations on the Microeconomic Level* (Yuhikaku, 1993), stresses the urgency of controlling the influx of unskilled migrant workers as a matter of policy. Ikuo Umebayashi, "An Overview of the Foreign Worker Problem and Some Proposals," Japan Center for Economic Research (JCER) Paper no. 13, May 1992, proposes a number of such policies.

[13] Kazuo Koike, "Aims of the Proposal for an Employment Permission System," *Jurist*, no. 909, June 1, 1988.

[14] Keiji Yonezawa (Councillor, Minister of Justice's Secretariat), "Problems with the Employment Permission System Advocated by the Ministry of Labor's Study Group on the Foreign Labor Problem" (mimeo).

[15] Tetsuo Yamazaki (Ministry of Justice, Immigration Bureau), "New Immigration Control for a New Age: A Response to the Foreign Worker Problem," *Kokusai Jinryu*, June 1990.

[16] Ministry of Justice, Immigration Bureau, ed., *Immigration Control in a Changing International Environment* (Ministry of Finance Publishing Office, 1986).

[17] Japan Association of Overseas Corporations, "International Survey of Visa Procedures and Residence Control" (Report by Research Committee on Response to Immigration Restrictions), July 1984.

[18] Tetsuo Yamazaki, "The New Immigration Control: The Revised Immigration Control and Refugee Recognition Law." In Yuji Koido, ed., *Foreign Workers: Policies and Issues* (Tax and Accountancy Association, July 1990).

[19] Japan Chamber of Commerce and Industry, "Chamber of Commerce Guidebook on Running Training Courses for Foreigners" (draft), March 1991.

[20] International Training Cooperation Organization, "Questions and Answers on Immigration Procedures for Foreign Trainees," December 1992.

[21] Networking on the acceptance of foreign trainees is moving steadily ahead in the private sector as well. IMM Japan (Medium and Small Business Foundation for Training International Staff) is one organization doing this systematically on a large scale. IMM Japan was established in December 1991, and started accepting trainees from Indonesia as a service to member businesses in June 1992.

Part II

A Work-and-Learn Program and Human Resource
Development

4

Proposal for a Work-and-Learn Program

1. The Concept

The "training" element of the Work-and-Learn Program I propose is defined as a process of acquiring skills through work experience. The word "training" is widely used in everyday speech, and its meaning tends to vary with the user and the context. Hence the above definition is meant to distinguish the word as I use it here from other common idiomatic usages.

A New Category of Residence Status
The best way of implementing the Work-and-Learn Program in its fullest form will be to partially amend the current Immigration Control Law and institute "work and learn" as a new category of residence status for foreigners.

The main object of the Work-and-Learn Program is to acquire skills, and my concept of "work and learn" is based on the recognition that skills can be acquired effectively only through actual work experience. There are basically no useful industrial skills that can be learned without first accumulating work experience. And work experience means actually, physically, working. The work element of "work and learn" of course differs from ordinary work in being designed for the acquisition of skills and directed solely to this end. Nevertheless it clearly has a work element. And insofar as trainees are doing actual work, they should naturally be paid a fair wage or suitably rewarded for their labor.

In line with this philosophy, and in recognition of the fact that the work experience of work-and-learn trainees does contain a work element, those for whom trainees do this work must fulfill their role as employers and pay trainees a market wage to compensate them fairly for their labor. But "work and learn" is also a process of acquiring skills. Employers taking part in the Work-and-Learn Program would be responsible for instructing trainees and helping them to obtain proper skills. Any special costs incurred in acquiring skills through the training process could be divided between the employer and the trainee.

To summarize, the new "work and learn" residence status would allow trainees seeking to acquire skills to obtain suitable work experience, and oblige those giving trainees this experience to pay them a fair wage as employers, in return for their labor.

Support for the Acquisition of Intermediate Skills
There ought to be some appropriate criterion for the skills acquired by trainees in the Work-and-Learn Program. And I think the skills best suited to the program are what we might call "intermediate" skills.

Intermediate skills pay an essential role in doing the work required by jobs in many industries; though they differ from one job to another, most such skills can be learned in two to three years.

Employers taking part in the Work-and-Learn Program would have to support trainees in acquiring intermediate skills appropriate to that particular industry or type of job, taking into account the wishes of the trainees themselves.

The process and methods of acquiring intermediate skills would probably differ with the industry, firm, or type of job, but whatever the job, trainees would start off at the "entry-job" level and gradually progress through a number of steps to more sophisticated work requiring higher levels of skills, before eventually mastering an intermediate skill. In other words, they would start out doing unskilled work, much like any new recruit without work experience or specialist knowledge; as they built up experience, they would move on to work demanding a higher level of knowledge and expertise.

The process of acquiring work skills by gradually progressing from unskilled to highly complex jobs is a universal practice in industry. But it is important that the Work-and-Learn Program not follow this process just because it is accepted practice. It should clearly describe the skills to be acquired, in the form of a manual, setting up authoritative standards that can be widely understood by employers and trainees alike. While Japanese workplaces do have well-established programs for acquiring skills through work experience, they are not clearly formulated, and in most cases the actual substance of the program is not immediately apparent to outsiders. It is important, then, to formulate a standard training procedure which can serve as a common basis for all trainees in the Work-and-Learn Program.

Japanese Language and Basic Skills a Major Prerequisite
If trainees are to acquire intermediate skills through the Work-and-Learn Program, they will need a working knowledge of the Japanese language and proficiency in certain basic skills.

Some ability to speak the language is an essential condition for living and working in Japanese society. And trainees must also be able to perform the basic tasks, whether calculation or construction, required by their particular professions. The Work-and-Learn Program sees these basic skills and abilities as a prerequisite for trainees, before they go on to learn intermediate skills through experience of increasingly more complex and sophisticated work.

Trainees should ideally acquire such basic skills and a minimum working knowledge of the language before they start to work in industry, since it is likely to prove difficult for many of the small businesses employing trainees to teach them in a systematic and orderly way on their own premises. A Work-and-Learn Program should set up what can be tentatively called Basic Education and Training Centers, where trainees will learn Japanese language and other basic skills. And since such education really amounts to basic educational aid, the Japanese government should make the initial investment in the Training Centers by mobilizing ODA funds and making use of its administrative leverage.

2. Organization and Management of the Work-and-Learn Program

The Work-and-Learn Program will be made up of a number of basic elements. There will be a legislative framework, agencies to implement the program, a system of qualifications for employers of trainees, an organization to run the program, basic education and training centers, and policies for repatriation, permanent residence, and naturalization.

(1) A New Work-and-Learn Residence System
Establishing "Work-and-Learn" Trainee Residence Status
To implement the Work-and-Learn Program in as complete and coherent a form as possible, "work-and-learn training" will have to be clearly stipulated under the law as a residence status for foreigners. Immigration regulations for such a residence status would clearly state that unskilled foreigners could reside in Japan for a fixed period of time for the purpose of acquiring intermediate skills under a work-and-learn program. The law would also make it incumbent on the management of firms taking in trainees, as their employers, to pay them a market wage for the work they do, and provide them with the necessary support and training to enable them to learn intermediate-level skills.

New legislation is not absolutely vital to realizing the objectives of the Work-and-Learn Program. The aims of the program could to some extent be achieved within the framework of the existing Immigration Control Law and the various laws and regulations already in force, provided the work-and-learn system and policies were correctly applied with definite objectives, and provided employers and ordinary people did their best to cooperate in the process. Nevertheless, a legally established trainee residence status would make it easier to implement the program effectively as well as making its aims more widely and accurately understood by society at large.

(2) Agencies Implementing the Program
The Work-and-Learn Program will be implemented by responsible organizations capable of fully realizing its aims; among these are corporations, small business organizations, and municipal authorities.

Under the Work-and-Learn Program, business proprietors will have the double-edged task of teaching trainees intermediate skills and at the same time providing them with work experience. One side of their role, giving trainees work experience, will be of definite benefit to employers as well, so here the aims of the program will probably be realized as a matter of course. But the other side of the employers' role, teaching trainees intermediate skills, will not always be of direct benefit to employers, and in many cases will saddle them with additional cost burdens. Furthermore, most lack the requisite knowledge, ability, and facilities to teach trainees a full range of intermediate skills.

To guarantee that trainees do actually acquire intermediate skills, employers will probably have to satisfy certain conditions before being allowed to participate. I will discuss these qualifications in more detail below, but basically participation should be open not just to individual companies but to small business organizations, local authorities like prefectural and municipal administrations, and other public bodies.

There is no reason why the Work-and-Learn Program should not be implemented by individual companies if they have the capacity and the facilities to realize its objectives and if they can be expected to carry out a proper training program, or can guarantee that they will. However, some small businesses will not have the resources to participate on their own, and in many cases will not be able to provide the necessary instruction and supervision to ensure that training is carried out properly. Yet one would not want to disqualify small companies from participating in the Work-and-Learn Program on these grounds alone. After all, such firms are very often managed by employers who are well placed to provide the program with work opportunities in industry, able to invest the necessary resources, and very eager to employ trainees. So to encourage and mobilize the enthusiasm, energy and resources of these small businesses and enable them to provide training in line with the aims of the Work-and-Learn Program, small-business organizations and local public authorities could take the responsibility in place of individual firms, and run implementation programs in which small firms could participate as members.

(3) Qualifications for Work-and-Learn Program Employers
Employers participating in the Work-and-Learn Program must fulfill at least three conditions if they are to realize the program's objectives. First, they must offer trainees a Career Development Program (CDP) and be able to give them proper support in acquiring intermediate skills. Second, they must pay trainees a reasonable wage. And third, they must be able to provide suitable accommodation.

Career Development
Career development programs (CDP) are discussed in more detail in the next chapter, but in simple terms they will make explicit, in the form of a program, the process by which trainees learn intermediate

skills while gaining work experience. Programs will lay out the process of skills acquisition, or career formation, in clear terms: how many months trainees will have in which to do a certain type of work, what type of work they can then graduate to, what knowledge they will gain along the way, and what skills they can expect to master. They will also set out trainees' work schedules, explain breaks in the schedule due to Japanese work practices, and set aside time for trainees to study those practices. The major condition for employers participating in the Work-and-Learn Program will be that they have such an explicitly defined career development program, and demonstrate the capacity to give trainees solid support in the acquisition of intermediate skills.

Appropriate Remuneration

The second condition employers in the Work-and-Learn Program must fulfil is that they pay trainees a fair wage. There may be concern over how to verify whether employers are paying fair wages or not, and whether trainees' pay is justified by their contribution, but this should be no more difficult than ensuring that employers respect the basic minimum wage in the ordinary domestic labor market. The important point is that the principle of equal pay for equal work is applied to foreign trainees just as it is to Japanese workers. Once that principle is established, the network of nearly 400 labor standards inspection offices throughout the country, coupled with the evidence of workers on site, will generally guarantee that trainees are paid proper wages.

Accommodation

The third major prerequisite for employers taking part in the Work-and-Learn Program is that they can provide trainees with suitable accommodation. Large corporations, well equipped with educational, training, and welfare facilities, will have little trouble fulfilling this condition, but small businesses, with their poorer resources, will often find it much more difficult. And finding accommodation may prove a particularly serious problem for small businesses in the big cities, where land prices and the cost of purchasing property are especially high. In cases where individual companies have difficulty providing accommodation, it may be possible to house trainees in some sort of communal housing facilities. But whatever accommodation is used, employers who cannot provide suitable housing for trainees should not be allowed to participate in the program.

While some individual companies may well be able to fulfill the above three conditions, many firms, particularly small ones, will simply not have the necessary capacity, facilities, or resources. But whatever the circumstances, employers unable to fulfill all three conditions cannot be allowed to join the program, since there is a danger they would not be able to realize the program's objective, which is that trainees should learn intermediate skills through work experience.

Small businesses with few resources or capabilities should obtain the support of local public bodies or industry organizations and work out some way to fulfill the requisite conditions by pooling their resources or sharing facilities. Hence, as we have seen, the agency implementing the Work-and-Learn Program will not always be an individual business: in some cases it may be more appropriate, or necessary, for responsible business organizations or public bodies to participate.

(4) Administrative Organization of the Program

If the Work-and-Learn Program is to operate in every part of the country, covering a wide range of industries and businesses, and at the same time be properly coordinated and run, it will need a highly competent and authoritative administrative organization. I have proposed for some time that a central organization to administer and run the program should be set up jointly by the government and private industry. It could perhaps be called the Work-and-Learn Employment Administrative Organization. Such an organization would have to perform many different functions, but here let us look at the seven most important.

(a) Research and Planning

The research and planning functions of the agency would come into play in the preparatory stages of the program's development. Some of these functions would be in particular demand in the earliest stages while others would be called upon continuously throughout the development of the program. The main role of the agency during the early planning stages would be to produce a master plan and a feasibility study.

In two areas of planning, there will be a logical need for surveys and research even after the program is underway. One area is studying the various Career Development Programs set up for trainees to acquire intermediate skills in different jobs and industries. Intermediate skills are those most in demand in industrial workplaces, and their nature is constantly changing in response to developments in products, services, and production technology. The agency would therefore have to study the situation constantly and revise CDP models appropriately or come up with new ones.

Another area will be examining how the intermediate skills obtained by trainees in Japanese workplaces can best be used when they return to their home countries. Although we cannot expect the skills mastered in Japan to be immediately or invariably usable in trainees' home countries, their work experience should insofar as possible be put to some effective use after they return home. Hence there will be a constant need for comprehensive and detailed studies comparing the skills in demand in trainees' home countries with the intermediate skills they are learning in Japanese industry.

(b) International Agreements

Trainees should be accepted into Japan in a systematic way under the provisions of international agreements drawn up in advance between Japan and the sender countries, in the same way as France and Germany have drawn up successive bilateral agreements with countries sending foreign workers. Such agreements could also be multilateral, but the experience of European and other industrialized countries that have admitted foreign workers in the past suggests that bilateral agreements with specific sender countries will be the pattern Japan adopts. Such agreements are formally signed by the governments of the countries concerned, but the process leading up to their signing involves an enormous amount of work, conducting all kinds of studies and negotiating with the sender countries. And the administrative organization, as the central repository for all the resources and information relating to the acceptance of trainees, would probably be in the best position to take on this preparatory work. It would be essential, of course, for the organization to maintain close contact with the Ministry of Foreign Affairs and the Ministry of Justice while the work was in progress.

(c) Regulating Total Numbers

There should naturally be a fixed upper limit on the number of trainees accepted by Japan, reflecting the state of the Japanese economy and labor market. Numbers could be limited to twenty or thirty thousand at the start of the program and eventually be expanded to several hundred thousand. Twenty or thirty thousand trainees would be nothing like enough to realize the Work-and-Learn Program's original objective of providing educational aid on a large scale, whereas an intake of several hundred thousand would make this possible.

From the point of view of industry, though, accepting large numbers of trainees may not seem particularly advantageous, since employers will have an obligation to help them acquire intermediate skills and cannot view the program simply as a means of obtaining unskilled labor. Nevertheless, a significant demand for trainees is expected in Japanese industry for some time to come, because they will be of use doing unskilled work for a certain period of time during the entry stage, and because employers face a long-term shortage of young Japanese workers, who are becoming increasingly selective in their career choices.

But while an upper limit of thirty thousand trainees spread through the whole country could probably be absorbed into society with scarcely a ripple, and would have little effect on the economy or the supply-and-demand balance of the labor market, things would not be so easy if several hundred thousand trainees were accepted. If they tended to gravitate to certain industries, types of jobs, or regions, this would materially affect society's ability to absorb them, and there would be a definite effect on the supply-and-demand balance of the labor market and the economy as a whole.

Hence the number of trainees accepted would have to be specifically limited and controlled. There would be "structural" limitations, in terms of Japan's social and institutional capacity to absorb them, and also a cyclical expansion and contraction of capacity due to fluctuations in the economy. Basically capacity would increase when the economy was doing well and decrease in times of recession. If Japan's capacity to absorb trainees does decline, it could lead to a deterioration in working conditions for marginal workers in the sectors where trainees tend to concentrate. Yet, once the Work-and-Learn Program has determined the number of trainees to be accepted, quotas cannot and should not suddenly be cut back simply because changes in the economy have reduced Japan's macroeconomic capacity to absorb trainees. Work-and-learn employment for trainees already accepted into the program should continue at least until projects already underway have been completed. On the other hand, if there is a decline in Japan's macroeconomic acceptance capacity, approval for new work-and-learn projects will obviously be less forthcoming.

Either way, there will clearly have to be controls on the total number of trainees accepted, in line with the country's institutional, structural, and cyclical capacity to accept them, and levels will have to be adjusted as that capacity fluctuates. Hence it will be another important function of the program's administrative organization to research and analyze the situation, estimate the capacity, and take the final decisions on how many trainees to admit.[1] This work will have to be very closely coordinated with national economic, industrial, and labor policy, and the organization will have to coordinate very closely with government departments like the Economic Planning Agency, the Ministry of Labor, and the Ministry of International Trade and Industry.

(d) Coordinating Distribution of Trainees within Industry

If controls are put on the number of trainees accepted, then, once the total quota has been determined, the most difficult problem will be how to distribute trainees among industries, regions, and businesses. In many different fields of industrial and business activity, the allocation of not just labor but output, scale of equipment, public investment, and basic resources like energy has become a very complex and serious problem. Resource distribution has frequently proved a headache to the administration due to fierce horizontal competitiveness between industries. But this problem of distribution is far from insoluble. We have seen from the way Japanese industry was able to adjust its production capacity in line with the restructuring of the economy, and restrain the volume of exports in response to trade friction, that it does have a considerable latent ability to carry out adjustments of market shares, with only indirect guidance from the government. By invoking this ability, therefore, the industrial sector should be able to distribute work-and-learn trainees on its own. With trainees, however, where it is a question not just of regulating numbers but of distributing people among industries as well, self-regulation may be much more difficult, particularly as many of the firms participating in the program will be small businesses incapable of the oligopolistic practices of large firms.

Still, this is less an essential difference than a problem of degree. And industry's ability to control the distribution of trainees will be an important key to implementing the Work-and-Learn Program in an ordered way. To ensure that trainees are properly allocated, the administrative organization will need the participation of private industry under a structure that fully delegates responsibility to industry rather than just reflecting its opinions and demands.

(e) Monitoring, Guidance, and Evaluation

One important function of the administering organization will be to monitor whether employers and the various other agencies implementing the Work-and-Learn Program are running it properly, in line with its objectives, and to give them guidance and advice concerning how the program should be run. We have seen that employers will be expected to fulfil three conditions: they must have a career development program, pay a fair wage, and provide accommodation. It will be the task of the administrative organization to verify that these conditions are being met, and to give firms the necessary advice and assistance to set up CDPs.

Another important function will be to set skills tests to evaluate whether trainees in the Work-and-Learn Program have mastered, or are learning, the requisite intermediate skills. These tests will be essential to finding out whether the program is working properly. Again, the organization should consider awarding certificates or qualifications to trainees who can show they have acquired a given level of skill. Where the Japanese labor market is concerned, this work will involve the Ministry of Labor's Labor Standards and Training divisions, while in implementing the tests the Labor Standards Inspection Offices and the nationwide network of Vocational Training Centers can be used. Hence close cooperation and liaison with the Ministry of Labor will be required.

(f) Consultation, Advice, and Support

In order for trainees to learn intermediate skills steadily and effectively under the Work-and-Learn Program, another important function of the administrative organization will be to provide a consultation service and give guidance and support when trainees encounter difficulties and problems during their stay. Again, this role can probably be carried out more effectively with the help of the counseling knowhow of the network of Public Employment Security Offices run by the Ministry of Labor.

(g) Acceptance, Repeating, and Repatriation

The final major role of the administering organization will be to handle the immigration and emigration of trainees and to organize repeat training programs.

The Work-and-Learn Program will accept trainees to work on projects lasting from two to five years, and trainees will be expected to return to their home countries immediately when their project is completed. One way of assuring that they have the means to return home might be to make trainees themselves save the money for their return travel expenses by depositing fixed-rate installment payments with the administering organization. Some such follow-up system will be needed to ensure that trainees are returned home in a smooth and orderly fashion.

Most trainees will be accepted under agreements with their own countries. The company, organization, or other body implementing the particular program will contact interested organizations and individuals in the sender countries, after which candidates will be specified. This process will demand an exchange of information between the two sides. But not all the agencies wishing to implement the program will possess sufficient information; indeed, most of the them will have hardly any information at all. So one important task will be to organize and supply proper information to companies and organizations wanting to take part, and to mediate in communications between them and the appropriate organizations in the sender countries.

Then there is the problem of trainees wishing to repeat. Naturally, trainees who have mastered an intermediate skill may wish to go on and learn more advanced skills. Hence, after completing their initial work-and-learn project, they will want to either rejoin the same project or switch to a different one—in other words, "repeat." And employers will tend to welcome this. After all, trainees who have learned skills on the employer's own premises will be tried and trusted, so it will be both natural and rational for employers to want trainees to continue if they can.

If trainees were permitted to repeat any number of times, however, they would eventually become, to all intents and purposes, permanent workers. And Japan would then be criticized both within the country and abroad unless it allowed the families of these workers to join them in Japan.

One way of dealing with the problem would be to prohibit trainees from "repeating" altogether, but not only would this be difficult from the practical point of view, it would not necessarily be the best way of providing people with a real education. If repeating is allowed, however, it will probably be hard to avoid the problems that occur when foreign workers settle in the country permanently.

I think that trainees should be allowed to repeat, and their families should be allowed to accompany them to Japan or join them later. After all, it is very much in line with the basic educational objectives of the program that trainees should go on to learn more advanced skills, and it is only natural that people should want to be with their families. But if trainees are allowed to repeat, we must expect some foreign workers and their families to stay in Japan and settle down in society. The question is whether Japanese society and the Japanese people will consent to this situation and whether they are prepared to accept foreign workers on a permanent basis. If they are not prepared to do so, the problem should be avoided by not allowing foreign workers or trainees into the country in the first place. To let them in and then refuse to let them stay or settle down is a very contradictory position.

3. Basic Education and Training Centers

Learning Japanese a Major Prerequisite
A vital prerequisite for foreigners wanting to work in Japan is that they learn Japanese. Not only will a knowledge of the language increase their understanding of the job and improve their efficiency; it will also be an essential condition for them to lead safe and comfortable lives in Japan.

If foreign workers are to understand their work correctly and do it properly, acquire knowledge and skills through working, and work in safety, it is very important that they learn Japanese. Workers unable to speak the language could be at a serious disadvantage. If they were cheated by their employers or were injured, they would not be able to appeal to the police. And they would find it difficult to make Japanese friends unless they could speak the language. Hence learning enough Japanese to get by in work and in everyday life is a major prerequisite for foreigners wishing to work in Japan.

Establishment of Basic Education and Training Centers

For a long time I have advocated that Japan set up what I have tentatively called Basic Education and Training Centers, to provide those wanting to come and work in Japan with the widest possible opportunity to learn the Japanese language. Such centers would constitute an important part—perhaps even the cornerstone—of the Work-and-Learn Program. Centers would be established in countries and regions sending workers to Japan, in easily accessible locations, to teach basic Japanese to as large a number of applicants as possible. Such facilities could also be set up in Japan by making use of the government vocational training and educational facilities all over the country, whose rate of use is declining, and the educational and training facilities of private companies.

Some jobs would require a relatively high standard of Japanese, while there would be others where trainees could get by with only the most basic knowledge of the language. Besides Japanese, the centers could usefully teach basic occupational skills where these were required. It would also be worthwhile giving trainees some orientation to Japanese society and culture.

ODA Funds for Japanese Language Teaching

The basic assistance in understanding Japan provided by the centers—Japanese language teaching, basic vocational skills and training, and an introduction to Japanese culture—constitutes educational aid, and Japan could probably best provide such assistance as part of its ODA (Official Development Assistance) program.

While ODA funds are put to many different uses, most of Japan's ODA budget is spent on developing the recipient country's "hard" facilities like agricultural and industrial infrastructure. However, "soft" aid like educational assistance is an important sector for future expansion, and aid for Japanese language instruction, basic education, and training for people wanting to work in Japan would be an important element in such educational assistance.

Japanese language and basic vocational skills are very useful abilities, not only to the foreign workers themselves but to those who employ them. Hence one could argue that people wanting to work in Japan should learn these skills at their own expense or, conversely, that their employers should pay for workers to acquire basic skills, since they reap the benefits.

There is of course some truth in this argument, and some trainees will no doubt acquire basic skills on their own initiative. But I maintain that the Japanese government—in other words, the taxpayers—should foot the bill for the language education of foreign workers, as part of the nation's educational ODA, for several reasons. First, there is the humane reason that the ability to speak Japanese will make living and working in Japan safer and more pleasant for foreign workers. Second, it will be of economic benefit, by helping to increase their work capacity and efficiency. Third, there is a public merit in that acquiring the ability to speak Japanese can be considered an investment in public goods. Clearly Japanese language ability does have the character of private goods, in being of benefit to both the individual trainees and their employers. But, in contrast to visiting foreign students, whose chief objective in coming to Japan is study and research, foreign workers come mainly to work, and therefore lack the freedom, ability, or inclination to master Japanese on their own time and at their own expense. Again, there is very little economic incentive for employers to help trainees acquire more than the most basic working knowledge of the language. But if the government, through foreign aid, were to support an overall improvement in the ability of foreign workers to speak Japanese, this would bring significant social benefits by increasing the effectiveness and improving the results of the Work-and-Learn Program. Hence, any investment in improving foreign workers' standard of Japanese could be seen as a public investment. Finally, an overall improvement in the ability of foreign workers to speak the language would have significant social and economic utility in the sense of raising the profile and usefulness of Japanese in international business and in workplaces.

One problem with using official aid to set up training centers is that many locally run Japanese schools are already in business in major cities in the foreign workers' home countries, and large-scale language teaching facilities set up with Japanese government aid could compete with these privately run businesses and deprive local people of their livelihoods. But the demand for Japanese language courses is expanding, so the market is not subject to zero-sum type competition. Furthermore, although the training centers will receive ODA support, they will be run as foundations, and should be able to coexist with local businesses, through tie-ups and other means. The most important thing is that the Japanese government and people recognize the public nature of Japanese as indispensable to working in Japan, and are willing to shoulder the burden of creating wealth in this intangible public asset.

Developing Skill in Teaching Japanese
Specialists have done considerable research into methods of teaching Japanese to foreigners, and a significant body of knowledge has now been accumulated.

Yet the state of development of the theory and methodology of teaching Japanese as a foreign language and the level of practical application of teaching methods still lag far behind the level of demand for Japanese teaching in the world today. In this respect Japanese is far behind English, French, Spanish, and German. The European languages have a very different background from Japanese in terms of their historical role in the spread of Western civilization, and there are facilities to teach them in every corner of the globe; they are also far ahead of Japanese in methodologies for teaching the language to foreigners. The historical background for Western language education may be a given condition, but people involved in Japanese language teaching should make every effort to close the gap in the development of methodology.

It is in Japanese language teaching in Japanese schools that a change in thinking is needed. In the Japanese education system it is the "mother tongue" that is taught in schools rather than "Japanese." The system teaches students the language as an integral part of their culture, to affirm their sense of shared identity as Japanese, but leaves out the concept of Japanese as a means of communication between people of different cultures. One cannot help thinking that this very biased attitude toward the Japanese language has helped obstruct attempts to come to grip with the problem of teaching Japanese to foreigners. It also seems that recent generations are no longer learning the Japanese language properly, whether as part of their culture or as a means of communication, and this is eroding the basis of clear and accurate communication even between Japanese. Developing methods of teaching Japanese to foreigners will therefore contribute greatly to the growth of accurate Japanese communication not only by foreigners but among the Japanese themselves.

Participation of Housewives in Japanese Language Teaching

One serious bottleneck confronting Japan in its efforts to promote the teaching of Japanese to foreign workers is the shortage of language teachers.[2]

Japan has only a limited number of specialist Japanese language teachers at present, but I think there is a very large number of potential teachers well capable of the task. This potential lies dormant in large numbers of housewives throughout the country, as is shown by their growing interest and enthusiasm and the recent increase in the number of housewives applying to obtain Japanese teaching qualifications.

If the ability of these housewives could be mobilized there would soon be an end to the shortage of Japanese language teachers. But certain environmental conditions will have to be met before housewives can participate positively and effectively. The first condition, as mentioned above, is an established concept of Japanese as a tool for communication, and a method of teaching the language to people with different languages and cultural backgrounds. Part of this process is to develop a basic form of Japanese that can be easily taught and understood. Second, Japanese housewives should be employed under short-term contracts, perhaps on a priority basis, to teach Japanese in the Basic Education and Training Centers to be established all over the world. At present a large number of housewives do teach Japanese as volunteers, which is admirable, but if a large-scale system is to be developed, they will have to be fairly rewarded according to their abilities, and this should act as a significant inducement for them to participate. To be paid several hundred thousand yen to teach Japanese for a few weeks in one of the centers around the world would surely be an attractive job prospect. Third, to enable housewives to work abroad, their husbands' working hours would have to be shortened and made more flexible to allow them to take over at home. Shortening working hours is very much in tune with the times, and if progress is made in shortening overtime hours, introducing flextime hours, and increasing the amount of paid holiday workers take, then housewives with the inclination and ability should be able to go abroad and teach without anxiety.

The significance of housewives teaching Japanese abroad is that their family-based values and view of the world tend to be more amenable to change, so they will get more out of the experience.[3] While the outlook of many working men tends to be limited by their company organizations, housewives have a freer and more individual attitude to life that is grounded in their contact with other people. Working in Asian countries as teachers will give housewives a serious, down-to-earth experience of living in another society. They will come back to Japan having had a taste of a foreign cultural environment, and will unconsciously reflect this experience in their everyday family life. And this in turn will influence the outlook of their children, gradually drawing them away from the world-view fostered by Japanese society, where people have tended to be isolated from the real world as though seeing it through a sheet of glass. Families will unconsciously start to reclaim what are basically their natural feelings toward other Asian people—and start seeing them with unprejudiced eyes.

When people live together with others and share their feelings of happiness and sadness, it becomes impossible to discriminate against others or look down on them. The experience enables people to relate to one another on the same level. Parents whose children have stayed with a family abroad and gotten close to them could hardly discriminate against those people. The best medicine for the groundless prejudice and discrimination that lies dormant in the Japanese is for everyone to get to know foreigners on an individual basis, and as family people. Hence I would expect the participation of housewives, whose identity is bound up most closely with the family, to have a strong positive effect.

4. The Significance of the Work-and-Learn Program

Aiming at Intermediate Skills

The Work-and-Learn Program seeks to enable the workers taking part to acquire intermediate-level skills. As we have seen, intermediate skills are those industrial skills that can be acquired through systematic work experience in a period of two to three years, and are the most important work skills in all industrial workplaces.

They are neither elementary nor advanced. Elementary skills are the minimum skills required to do work that any unskilled new recruit can do straight off with just a little instruction. While they differ from one type of job to another, they can generally be learned with a few hours to a few days of practice. Most unskilled work or manual labor falls into this category. And the skills required by the jobs in which most of Japan's illegal foreign workers are now working are elementary skills of this kind.

Advanced skills, on the other hand, while they also vary with the type of job, take at least three to five years of training and practice to master. Most jobs demanding a high level of expertise require advanced skills. The Ministry of Labor's Skills Development Bureau currently conducts skills tests for 133 different job types, and passing tests in most of these skills requires a training period of three to five years, sometimes longer. The skills certified by these tests are typical of what I refer to here as advanced skills. Intermediate skills lie somewhere between these two extremes. They are not the kind of manual skills that anyone can do straight away with a minimum of instruction, but neither do they require years of hard training. They are skills that any worker can master with two to three years of systematic training and work experience, and they are also the most necessary and useful skills for productive activity in industry.[4]

In-house Training, the Forte of Japanese Corporations
As we have seen, the main object of the Work-and-Learn Program is that Japanese companies employ unskilled foreign workers and train them in intermediate skills inside the company. This is very different from the current situation, in which nearly all illegal foreign workers are being made to do "unskilled" jobs. The great majority of employers tend to exploit them as manual labor, since they are willing to do the unskilled and unpleasant jobs that Japanese workers are reluctant to do. Hence employers seldom even think of teaching them skills.

But the behavior of most employers today is actually quite estranged from traditional attitudes. It has always been the forte of Japanese corporations to take in unskilled workers and forge them into skilled workers who are at the same time very much the products of their company. It is this attitude toward employment that lies behind the predilection of Japanese firms for taking in new graduates.

They tend to dislike workers with past employment histories. The use of the discriminatory term "halfway recruit" for an employee who has worked elsewhere shows such attitudes are still prevalent today. But employing new graduates, whether from high school or university, generally means employing people with no skills or training—in other words, untrained recruits.

The reader should note that I use the word "untrained" rather than "unskilled," which conjures up the image of a person who works in an unskilled job and will continue to do so for life. In societies where there are few opportunities for upward social mobility, and in authoritarian countries with a stubbornly hierarchical social structure, there are in fact many workers who remain in unskilled jobs all their lives.

Everybody starts out unskilled. Then, if they are given the opportunity for proper education and training, people build up work experience and become skilled. A new Japanese university graduate, for instance, may have all sorts of potential abilities but in labor terms is an untrained recruit like any other. But by working in industry he or she will build up experience and eventually acquire the knowledge to become a skilled and trained worker.

Hence Japanese corporations deserve credit for training unskilled recruits to become fully trained and skilled workers, which does not happen in countries with class societies. It is true the Japanese system is based on the premises of a relatively uniform labor pool and the practice of lifetime employment. This may be why workers make such strong efforts to compete with each other, attempting to "steal each other's accomplishments," and why skills have tended to be transmitted and acquired autonomously without employers having to go out of their way to teach them. But skills cannot be formed out of nothing. Training cannot take place where there is no base for it. While skills may not have been very clearly delineated, Japanese industry has a long tradition of forming and transmitting work skills of a high order. It is just that the processes and mechanisms of transmitting and acquiring intermediate skills have not been specifically spelled out, since the workers have always been Japanese, brought up to speak the same language, and employed under a lifetime system as comrades "eating rice out of the same bowl."

I only want to press one point here—that these fine work practices should not be left vague and undefined but brought out into the open in the form of a system with its own set of rules. Japanese companies have proved themselves very proficient at the in-house training of Japanese workers, so one wonders why the same methods cannot be applied to foreign workers. This could easily be done if just a little initiative were expended on clarifying the system and its rules.

As we have seen, however, current trends in the employment of foreign workers give cause for great concern. Most employers taking on unskilled foreign workers treat them as a different sort of labor from Japanese workers and do not even consider giving them the in-house training that Japanese companies have traditionally been so good at. Nevertheless, in simple labor terms foreign workers are in no way different from their trained Japanese counterparts in terms of their inherent abilities. Both "untrained" and foreign workers differ from Japanese only in their language and customs.

As I pointed out earlier, the Work-and-Learn Program does not target foreign workers who only want a temporary income, but those who come to Japan to learn skills. Hence it is important not only to provide these workers with the opportunity to learn the language before they come to Japan, but to incorporate them into the Japanese in-house training system which has traditionally been such a unique strength of the Japanese company. Companies will have to make the institutional changes that will enable them to make rational choices in accepting foreign workers.

A System in Which Properly Motivated Employers Can Participate
The Work-and-Learn Program seeks to enable properly motivated employers to employ foreign workers openly as trainees.[5] A system that looks good on paper but does not work in practice, or one that can be abused by dishonest employers, will do more harm than good. Of course it will not be easy to design, operate, or maintain such a practicable system. But it is vital that efforts be made to design a system more in line with the aims of the program, and to offer constructive criticisms of the deficiencies in the real system from this perspective.

As I mentioned earlier, the "study and training" system in which foreigners can enroll under the current Immigration Control Law suffers from problems on two counts. First, it is difficult to put into practice, and second, it is open to abuse by unscrupulous employers.

Looking at the practicality of the system first, the requirement that firms devote more than a third of the training period to study, and other conditions imposed by the current law, are, as we have seen, so at odds with the actual situation in real jobs as to effectively prevent small businesses, which would otherwise be very well placed to accept trainees, from participating in the system. The main requisites for firms taking part in the program should be that they are technically capable of participating and that there is at least some economic incentive for them to do so. But the present rules make it difficult for small businesses on both counts, effectively barring many of these firms from the system.

The technical difficulties for small businesses in industries where trainees could be accepted center on their resentment of the long study period, which takes up the first four to eight months of a course of training. What actually happens in most skilled jobs is that skills are formed gradually: trainees are launched into work experience with only a little guidance at first, and then knowledge is systematically introduced as the skills become more complex. In other words, the process of acquiring skills is a step-by-step one in which trainees progress by stages from the elementary entry-job level up to the level of intermediate skills. Designing a study and training program that matches the actual situation, therefore, will mean removing the condition that the initial one third of the training period be given over to study.

The economic difficulty for small businesses is that, even where firms conduct training in advanced skills which do necessitate a four- to eight-month study period, this does not offer much economic advantage to the employer. Not only is the study period too long and the costs too high, but employers cannot recover the costs they incur in the subsequent short period of "work training." Again, there are basically not very many advanced skills that require such long periods of study, and jobs demanding these skills tend to be filled with ordinary Japanese workers, so there is little excess demand in the market and no need to rely on foreigners to fill the gap.

Companies must essentially be economically viable. They are not constituted so as to engage in social work or altruistic activities. In other words, they cannot do work that does not pay for itself and bring some sort of return. They can only contribute to society when such work makes broad economic sense.

Many small companies clearly have a strong need to employ foreign workers, not only because it is more profitable economically but because they are willing to do jobs that Japanese workers will not take, in manual-labor sectors involving no education or training costs. In the current Japanese labor market it is an unfortunate fact, as I have repeatedly pointed out, that the great majority of employers use foreigners to do such manual work in the knowledge that they are working illegally.

This arrangement benefits illegal employers in a one-sided way and should not be condoned. But on the other hand, unless a program brings some economic benefit to properly motivated employers, it will prevent them from participating and end up being wholly ineffective. Not only this, but illegal employers will continue to flout the law in their single-minded pursuit of economic profit, causing widespread social damage as the number of illegal workers increases.

To absorb foreign workers who wish to learn skills under employers who respect the law, therefore, will require a training program designed to bring some advantage to these properly motivated employers. It is an undeniable reality that from the employers' point of view, the more unskilled and manual the work is, the more it profits them. While not all of their demands can be met, some compromise must be worked out that enables their interests to be accommodated.

Work-and-learn employment could constitute such a point of rational compromise since it would be conditional on trainees acquiring intermediate skills as advocated by the Work-and-Learn Program. Under the program, employers will be able to bring in foreign trainees at the entry-level job stage. And since it will be a prerequisite that trainees have acquired a working knowledge of the language by completing a basic education and training course, the employer will need only to give them a minimal amount of training to enable them to learn the elementary skills to do the job. But this advantage to the employer will bring with it the obligation to guarantee that trainees learn intermediate-level skills within the two- to three-year training period. Employers who do not fulfill this obligation will not be permitted to employ work-and-learn trainees.

In other words, the Work-and-Learn Program will bring definite advantages both to employers and to the country in a broad political sense—with repercussions on international relations as well. And it is this common advantage that makes the program so practicable.

Advantages for Work-and-Learn Graduates

So far we have looked at the significance of the Work-and-Learn Program mainly from the aspect of employers and the administration;

but let us now consider it from the point of view of the trainees themselves.

To participate in the Work-and-Learn Program trainees must first learn a certain amount of Japanese and the basic knowledge they will need for their training course, at one of the Basic Education and Training Centers either in their home country or in Japan.

After completing this basic training they will start the process of working and learning, gaining proficiency in intermediate skills while working for one of the many employers participating in the program. Employers taking part in the Work-and-Learn Program, as we have seen, will have had to fulfill at least three conditions.

First, they will pay trainees a proper market wage for the work they do. Second, they will provide suitable housing. Third, they will have an appropriate Career Development Program to teach trainees intermediate skills. Trainees taking part in the program under such employers should therefore come out of the experience with quite favorable impressions.

First, since they will have acquired a basic working knowledge of the language in order to be able to work in Japan, they should have had little trouble in their everyday lives. Being able to interact with the people around them and make themselves understood, they should also have made some Japanese friends.

Second, since they will have been paid the same wages as Japanese people doing the same work, trainees who have lived fairly frugally will have managed to save or send home a considerable amount of money. Those who have stayed in Japan and saved for a few years should have been able to build up the funds to set up small-scale businesses or companies when they return.

Third, since they will have been provided with decent accommodation, they will not have experienced too much difficulty, or been discriminated against, in searching for a place to live. Properly housed, they will have been able to live relatively stress-free and healthy lives in Japan.

Fourth, and most importantly, the CDP will have enabled them to learn intermediate skills that will be of real use to them in the workplace. These skills may not be immediately usable in the trainees' home countries, but they will have been able to pick up some basic knowledge and also learn something of the way of thinking, attitudes, and skills of professionals and skilled workers in industry. They will know how to carry out responsible jobs, what skills are demanded by industry, and what it means to run a small business. And they should be able to apply these skills and attitudes as capable professionals in their own countries.

If tens, or possibly hundreds, of thousands of people with such favorable impressions of Japan are returning every year to the neighboring Asian countries, their presence is sure to go a long way toward building understanding and forming links between those countries and Japan.

For individual Japanese businesses, too, it will be encouraging to know that they have large numbers of such allies in neighboring countries. High Japanese wage levels and the consequent high production costs mean that however small firms are, they must rationalize by transferring their productive activity overseas where production costs are lower. The transfer of production overseas has now acquired an irreversible momentum, as we can see from the increasing level of Japanese direct investment. And one of the greatest obstacles to this internationalization of business activity is the problem of communication between people in the recipient countries and Japanese managers, supervisors, and technicians. Of course the employees of Japanese firms making direct investments overseas seldom speak the languages of these countries and are far from fluent in English, which is the effective international language. But people in the recipient countries are almost entirely ignorant of Japanese as well. So even if they can communicate on a superficial level through English, there is still a large gap between the two sides in terms of their everyday assumptions, which are rooted in their different customs and values, and they still have significant problems in making themselves fully understood. Hence the presence in neighboring countries of large numbers of people with experience of the Work-and-Learn Program, familiar with life in Japan, and speaking the vernacular Japanese of the workplace will be an immense help in the development of Japanese firms overseas.

A Little More Effort Will Solve the Problem
As we have seen, the Work-and-Learn Program can only be realized in its complete form if the current Immigration Control Law is partially amended to include "training" as a new category of residence status, properly established under the law.

Even under the existing system and legal framework, however, the Work-and-Learn Program can accomplish its basic aims to a large extent provided there is a deeper awareness of the significance of the problems of foreign workers, and provided the Japanese government, employers, and the country as a whole make just a little more effort to resolve them. I would like to close this chapter by summarizing what extra efforts might be made by the government, by employers, and by the Japanese people under the present situation.

The approach of government policy up to now has been wide of the mark. It is not that the thinking behind the current Immigration Control Law or its main provisions, as revised at the end of 1989, represent the wrong approach to a solution. What has happened is that the doors have been opened wider, allowing foreigners with relatively high-level skills and knowhow to work in Japan more easily while preventing people with no such skills from entering the country for the purposes of employment. As I have pointed out, though, difficulties remain in the middle ground of a study and training system for unskilled foreigners. Hence there is a pressing need to rectify the undesirable present situation in which, due to these and other institutional faults, most correctly motivated employers are barred from participating in the training system while unscrupulous employers profit by exploiting the loopholes in the law.

The government has not entirely ignored these problems. In October 1991, the International Foundation for Cooperation in Training was inaugurated and started preparatory work on improvements to the system; and in December 1991, as we have seen, the Third Administrative Reform Council proposed the establishment of a skills work-training (*ginō jisshu*) system that comes one step closer to the type of system I have advocated for some years.

But if we take the present situation as a given and focus on that framework for the time being, the government can contribute greatly to improving the situation by expending just a little extra effort. Let us look at two examples of how it could do this.

First, it could spell out to employers wishing to take part in the training system the intermediate skills trainees are expected to learn in different industries and types of job, and drive home to them the objectives of the system. As I have explained, despite the fact that these intermediate skills play such an established role in the Japanese labor market, neither their content nor their acquisition have ever been clearly set out. The government should therefore take immediate steps to codify the content of these skills and the process of acquiring them, and set up standards of qualification for the five hundred or so main types of job that require intermediate skills. It should then make sure this information is thoroughly understood both by employers and by people at all levels of society.

Second, the concept, design, implementation, running, and maintenance of a study and training system, or work-and-learn program, for unskilled foreign workers is actually a very complex business involving an enormous amount of work, which is very time-consuming and demands considerable ability and dedication. It was to cope with this work that the government set up the International Foundation for Cooperation in Training, but this organization does not yet have even a tenth of the capacity it will need, in terms of staff and funding, to take on the job of running a full-scale program. Considering the importance of the foreign worker question to Japan's future, the nation cannot afford to rely solely on small contributions from the private sector to accomplish the task. Indeed, the scale of the task is such that the government should seriously consider setting up an independent ministry with sole responsibility for foreign workers. In any case it should waste no time in drawing up a properly thought-out policy. It should establish some sort of official organization to tackle the work, allocate an annual budget in the tens of billions of yen, and mobilize the private sector to cooperate as far as it can.

Next, let us look at what employers can do. Even under the present system, as I have pointed out, employers could do three things.

First, they could pay a larger training allowance for the actual work done by trainees. As I have stressed, employers should basically pay a market wage appropriate to the work trainees do, whether it is for training purposes or not. While this policy has not been adopted by the current study and training system, employers can still pay a training allowance close to the actual market wage. Hence foreigners who work during their training course could be remunerated at close to the market rate, if employers would compensate for the failings of the system by paying them an appropriate allowance.

Second, employers could provide suitable housing. Employers who seek to provide proper training, as opposed to those deliberately employing illegal workers as cheap labor, do seem to pay some attention to accommodation conditions, but they should try to apply such standards as a maximum of two people to a room.

Third, employers could make more effort to ensure that trainees learn intermediate skills. They should be expected to specify a career development program for acquiring such skills and to ensure that trainees progress from elementary to intermediate skills in accordance with the program.

If employers take the initiative and make such efforts on their own account, then, even under the present training system, the aims of the Work-and-Learn Program I have advocated will come close to being realized.

Enlisting Local Support

I have listed the efforts which I think the government and employers should make, but it is local authorities and implementing agencies in local areas that can really help to get results in the training of unskilled foreigners. In addition, the key to the success of a training program lies in the understanding and support of the Japanese people.[6]

Central government can prescribe the general legal provisions and set up the institutional framework, but it is at the local level that training will actually take place. Local authorities at the prefectural and municipal levels will be able to participate in the development of the Work-and-Learn Program, and could provide leadership in many areas.[7]

Under the legal framework of the existing training system, local authorities already play a significant role in the promotion of training. They assist with the content and the funding of training prgrams developed by small business groups, and on occasion implement training programs themselves.

Such involvement at the local level is very important because each local area supports its own community, within which there are very close ties between the firms employing trainees and the organizations concerned with the program, so that long-term relationships are formed very easily. In close-knit communities of this kind it is very difficult for firms to behave irresponsibly, as they can easily do in the big cities where they are shielded by a cloak of anonymity. To live and do business in a local community where people are bound together by long-term ties, it is vitally important to be trusted. To act in a way that destroyed that trust could jeopardize one's whole position in the community. In other words, a very strict autonomous mechanism operates in local communities, whose members constantly hold each other in check and under surveillance.

While it cannot be denied that this pattern of relationships tends to exclude outsiders, it does function extremely effectively to protect properly motivated employers and cut the ground from under those out to abuse the system. This characteristic of regional Japanese society—the closeness of relationships and absence of anonymity—should therefore be taken full advantage of as the social base for a properly run training system.

Finally, I would like to emphasize that the most important factor in the smooth and proper development of a training program is that each individual Japanese should appreciate the importance of the foreign worker problem and understand that, if foreigners are to be admitted into Japanese society, they must be welcomed as equal human beings.

Notes

[1] Of equal importance to setting appropriate limits on the total numbers of foreign workers accepted is the task of instituting an employment introduction system overseas. The Ministry of Labor has recently begun studying how this might be done. Working Group on a Regulatory System for Overseas Labor Supply and Demand, "Possible Ways of Setting Up an Employment Introduction System Overseas," Ministry of Labor, Employment Security Bureau, Office of Private Sector Supply and Demand Regulation, February 16, 1993.

[2] There are approximately 8,900 teachers who specialize in teaching Japanese to foreigners in Japan, according to a survey carried out by the Agency for Cultural Affairs at the end of 1991.

[3] For example, the International Internship Program conducts volunteer activities all over the world with the aim of introducing Japanese culture. Over the last ten years the program has sent several thousand housewives and other volunteers overseas to teach Japanese language and other aspects of Japanese culture, with notable success.

[4] A useful description of the organization and functioning of the training system is given in Koichiro Imano and Hiroki Sato, *Foreign Trainees: Purpose and Functioning of the Training System* (Toyo Keizai Shimposha, 1991).

[5] Surveys of the employment of foreign workers show they are engaged in

important work and form the mainstay of the workforce at many medium and small businesses. Takeshi Inagami, Yasuo Kuwahara, et al., *The Increasingly Strategic Importance of Foreign Workers to Medium and Small Businesses* (Medium and Small Business Research Center, 1991). Tokyo Metropolitan Labor Research Institute, "The Employment of Foreign Workers in the City of Tokyo," March 1991. Medium and Small Business Managers' Compensation Association, "A Report on Foreign Workers: The Foreign Worker Problem and the Situation and Level of Awareness among Medium and Small Business Managers," May 1990.

[6] Kazuaki Tezuka et al., eds., *Foreign Workers and Local Authorities* (Akashi Shoten, 1992), is a report on the international symposium on the issue hosted by Kanagawa Prefecture, and suggests many areas where local authorities, which come into direct contact with foreign workers, can play a potentially major role.

[7] Masaaki Yorimitsu ["The Foreign Worker Problem on the Local Level: The Debate on How Local Authorities Should Deal with the Problem," Labor Market Research Committee; "Changes in the Economic Structure and the Labor Market," Tokei Kenkyukai (Statistical Research Association), 1991] advocates the need to develop integrated policies and services at the local level.

5

The Formation of Intermediate Skills

Throughout the discussion of the Work-and-Learn Program in the previous chapters, I have stressed both the importance of intermediate skills formation and the need for a plan setting out clear programs that will help trainees to acquire these skills. In this chapter, I would like to explain in more detail just what intermediate skills are, and what programs for the formation of intermediate skills might look like.

1. The Importance of Intermediate Skills

Intermediate skills are the skills in greatest demand in the average workplace. Neither elementary nor advanced, they are of such a level that workers who have mastered them can safely be left to work unattended.

They are not especially sophisticated skills, and do not require the mastery of inordinately complex or precise tasks. Neither are they particularly specialized in nature. They differ, for example, from the skills needed to deal with accidents or other emergencies on an occasional basis. Really specialist skills of this type are best delegated to people specifically trained to perform them.

Intermediate skills are the skills that most workers in industry are required to master as part of their jobs. Most such skills take somewhere between two and five years of work experience to learn.

Since people have to master these skills in order to be able to work effectively, they tend to pick them up naturally in the course of their work experience. In a sense, therefore, the labor market forms intermediate skills automatically. Nevertheless, people can still learn skills more effectively through a planned and systematic program.

Such programs are likely to be particularly effective for foreign workers. Most foreign workers will not remain in Japan indefinitely, and it is therefore important both to them and to their employers that they master a certain level of skills in an orderly and purposeful way within the limited time available. Obviously, since foreign workers are handicapped by their poorer grasp of the language, they will benefit from planned and systematic study along with the natural process of picking up skills through work experience.

Let us refer to such planned and systematic programs for the acquisition of intermediate skills as "career development programs" (CDPs). Intermediate skills CDPs will not only be of use to foreign workers but will also be very beneficial, in view of the future prospects of the Japanese labor market, to various segments of the Japanese workforce. We will consider their various benefits in more detail later on.

Intermediate Skills Poorly Defined

Up to now there has been no real definition of intermediate skills, nor even any discussion of what they are or how they can be acquired. Workers have tended to form these skills automatically, through their work experience, in response to the needs of their particular workplaces.

Although intermediate skills are vital to industry, there has never been any perceived need to specify the process of their formation, due to the traditional employment system and employment practices prevailing in the Japanese labor market. At the risk of oversimplifying, we can say that the Japanese labor force under the traditional employment system consists of a core of long-term regular workers and a periphery of temporary workers and part-timers. But there has never been any need to define the process or standards of intermediate skills formation for either of these groups.

Members of the core workforce under the lifetime employment system must eventually acquire high-level skills and expertise. But they seek to acquire these skills through their own efforts rather than by relying on others. In the world of the traditional Japanese crafts it was said that "crafts have to be stolen"—a statement that applies equally well to these core workers. The system requires them to learn skills in secret, through their own individual efforts, and then to use those skills to gain the upper hand over their colleagues in the promotion stakes. Paradoxically, so long as the workers themselves are motivated to acquire skills in this way, any overt attempt to teach skills would probably be counterproductive.

Part-timers, meanwhile, only work on a temporary basis or to earn extra income, and are not basically interested in mastering skills to begin with. Hence the Japanese employment system and the structure of the workforce have tended to obviate the need to define any process of intermediate skill formation or indeed to teach skills in any way. Instead, skills were picked up naturally in the workplace as the need arose.

But the advent of foreign labor has completely changed the situation. Since the abilities of foreign workers have to be drawn out, developed, and put to use within a short time span, there is now a clear need to define intermediate skills and teach them in an organized and systematic way.

There are also other reasons for defining intermediate skills more accurately. The influx of foreign workers may have spotlighted the problem, but changes are also occurring at a deeper, underlying level, due to the growing importance of the service industries and to changes in the structure of the labor force.

The relative increase in the size of the tertiary industries and the diversification of the labor force have increased the flexibility of the previously very rigid employment system, and encouraged greater labor mobility. These structural changes mean that workers can no longer be expected just to pick up skills automatically through the lifetime employment system. Instead, intermediate skills will increasingly have to be formed in a systematic manner under specific programs tailored to a more mobile workforce. I think this will apply to the younger segments of the Japanese workforce in even greater measure than it applies to Japan's foreign workers today.

What Are Intermediate Skills?

Let us clarify once more what we mean by intermediate skills. The skills we are talking about here are not the basic skills that workers have to learn immediately when they start working, just in order to do the job. They do require a certain amount of training and practice to master. But neither are they the specialized skills possessed only by a limited number of experts. Intermediate skills have to be acquired by most workers in the average industrial workplace, in the regular course of carrying out their duties in a responsible manner.

The specific nature of intermediate skills of course varies with the industry and type of job, but they are basically skills that can be learned with two to three years, or five years at the most, of practical work experience. The important point is that they are practical skills, and they have to be mastered before workers can take full responsibility for their jobs. The specific nature of these intermediate skills has to be defined individually for each separate skill. Naturally the type of training required will also vary from one skill to another, as will the length of time required, the amount of practice, and the standards by which proficiency in the skill is judged.

We can get some idea of the nature of these skills by looking at a few examples. Let us take the assembly of plywood forms in the construction industry. This involves putting the forms together according to the measurements on a plan, and then pouring in concrete mixed with gravel, to construct the foundations for houses and the walls of concrete buildings. Just assembling the forms in line with the measurements, and mixing and pouring the concrete into them, is a basic skill that any construction worker has to learn, and can master without much difficulty.

But this basic skill will not enable a worker to build a concrete wall that is flawless. Cracks may appear, and water may leak in if the wall is part of an underground foundation. Such defects frequently appear around joins in the concrete where work has been interrupted. The finer skills, like making allowances for the speed of hardening of the concrete, and making seamless joins, take a certain amount of experience and judgment. If the judgment is faulty, or the timing is wrong, a concrete wall will be defective. And we could hardly say that the worker was qualified to take full responsibility for the job.

Overcoming such problems and avoiding mistakes does not necessarily require specialist skills or knowhow. But it does require at least a couple of years of experience in which to refine the skill. Only after a worker has reached such a level can he or she safely be entrusted to do the job unattended.

Let us now turn to another example—that of a fast-food outlet. The work at such stores involves many different kinds of skill. There are a number of different types of work to be done: serving customers, cooking, operating the till, bookkeeping, dishwashing, cleaning, stock control, and purchasing.

Which of these jobs could be done by a completely unskilled worker without training? Virtually anyone could work in the kitchen as a dishwasher, serve tables, or work as a cleaner, even if they could not communicate very well. Even high-school students can serve customers with just a little instruction. But work like bookkeeping, stock control, purchasing, and materials distribution management demand a higher level of knowledge and a certain amount of training. The shop manager, meanwhile, has to oversee the whole combination of jobs, check on the progress of work, and lead and coordinate the other workers in achieving given management objectives.

Which of these jobs correspond to intermediate skills? If we define intermediate skills as those which enable people to do a job unsupervised, strictly speaking the only job that really qualifies for the title is that of shop manager. Most shop managers in Japan tend to be university graduates who have undergone about three years of training. It is probably unreasonable to expect a foreign worker with limited Japanese language ability to cope with the job of shop manager. Yet, clearly, washing up and cleaning can hardly be considered jobs whose holders could safely be left in charge of the workplace. A worker would at least need to have some idea of what the management and running of a fast-food store entailed, and would have to have at least some experience of all the various types of job involved. This would probably demand experience at serving customers, distributing materials, and bookkeeping.

Before being left to work unattended, a worker would need to master about two thirds of the work that someone would need to experience in order to qualify as a shop manager. The worker would then have a basic grasp of fast-food store management, and would have a certain intuitive sense of the job that would prove useful if, for example, he or she chose to set up a business in the service sector after returning home. The intermediate skills we are talking about are skills of this level.

Intermediate Skills Career Development Programs
Career development programs for intermediate skills would enable the formation of these skills in an organized and systematic manner. Such programs would help to develop skills that could form the basis of life-long careers.

In the Japanese labor market intermediate skills tend to be formed "naturally" through work experience, and the process has never been clearly defined. CDPs would attempt to describe the formation process clearly, defining in simple terms the elements that go to make up intermediate skills, the nature of the experience and practice needed to acquire them, and each of the steps in the formation process. Once CDPs are clearly defined in this way, it should be possible to evaluate intermediate skills based on the programs, and to test them with reference to fixed standards.

The complex of intermediate skills that CDPs will help to define exists in an intermediary zone between the "inner" and "outer" labor markets. Basically the inner labor market is that contained within large corporate organizations. Here labor is distributed and work allocated less through the competitive price mechanism of the market than through the rules of personnel management, wage systems, and labor-management negotiations. Workers are recruited, trained, and assigned to jobs within the corporate organization, then gradually move upward through its ranks.

In this "internal market," skills are formed through work experience and the corporation's own educational and training system, in line with the aims of corporate activity. Hence skills are internalized within organizations, and lose their currency in the outside market as well as their direct link to market prices. Workers remain within the same organization for the whole of their working lives and are circumscribed by its rules, so intermediate skills represent no more than one phase of their careers. And since all they are required to do is practice the skills, there is no particular need to define them in a way that outsiders can understand.

In the outer labor market, on the other hand, neither workers nor skills are contained within large corporate organizations. Outside the corporate world, the decisive factors that influence the allocation of work and the connections between workers and their jobs are the supply and demand balance and market prices.

The temporary and part-time workers we considered above belong to this outer labor market. But it also contains highly skilled and specialized workers, including individual workers—qualified professionals like lawyers, tax accountants, doctors, and architects; specialists who work on their own in fields like finance, technology, and the arts; and highly skilled craftspeople such as carpenters or chefs.

Since market value plays a decisive role in these professions, due to the forces of supply and demand and to professional ranking, skills are evaluated by strict, clearly defined, and inescapable standards, which professionals become aware of in the course of their work. The process of skill formation is also clearly defined—whether in the apprentice arrangements of the traditional crafts or in the state examination system for professional qualifications.

CDPs for intermediate skills would occupy a sort of middle ground between the different processes of skill formation that characterize the inner and outer labor markets. The process would neither be as closed as in the inner labor market nor as strict as in the highly skilled professions or the traditional crafts. What is important is that the process of formation of these most useful of industrial skills should be clearly defined in a way that can readily be understood by all.

Present Skills Testing: Narrow and Elitist

Japan already has a public system for evaluating skill proficiency. The Ministry of Labor conducts tests in cooperation with prefectural and local authorities and organizations such as professional skills development associations.

The system is basically a good idea, but as applied to the kind of intermediate skills we have been looking at, the current tests are inadequate on two counts. First of all, too few skills are covered, and they are too narrowly spread among a small number of industries and professions.

The present official skills testing system covers 133 skills selected "from among those with the highest perceived need, subject to overall consideration of their importance to the national welfare and the national economy, demands from interested parties, the numbers of workers involved, and the status of educational and training programs." However, the selection is heavily biased in favor of the construction industry and parts of the traditional manufacturing sector, and very few tests are conducted for the vast range of skills in the service industries and the high-technology field which has expanded so rapidly in recent years.

Not only do the official skills tests cover too few intermediate skills, but the standard is excessively high. It is as though they are intended to confer honors on master craftspeople rather than to test the sorts of skills that people have to master in order to work effectively and responsibly in industry.

For example, the system conducts first- and second-grade skills proficiency tests for carpenters. But to pass even the second grade—which ought to correspond to intermediate level—requires complete mastery of a wide range of knowledge and techniques. The written examination tests candidates on:

(1) Building procedures: basic theory of the types, characteristics, structure, and fixtures of wooden buildings; types, characteristics, and structural dynamics of other types of buildings.

(2) Measuring skills: basic principles of measurement, use of the carpenter's square, measuring edges and squares, and allotment of timber.

(3) Building methods: types of tools and machines used in carpentry and their methods of use, planning for wooden building construction work, methods of temporary construction work, taking levels, layout and use of the inking string, methods of foundation work, carpentry methods, types and methods of carpentry-related work, protective techniques, and repair of wooden buildings.

(4) Materials: types, standards, qualities, and uses of building materials.

(5) Draftsmanship: drawing of plans for wooden buildings.

(6) Building laws and regulations; Building Standards Act and other building regulations.

(7) Health and safety: specific knowledge of health and safety issues.

There is also a practical examination in which candidates have to demonstrate their ability in carpentry, level-taking, layout and marking with the inking string, woodworking, and balancing.

A carpenter in overall charge of building a wooden house would certainly need to have a good grasp of all these skills. But the same is not necessarily true of a semi-skilled worker at a construction site under the supervision of a head carpenter. In the case of the building trade, then, it would be useful to identify a number of intermediate skills at a level slightly below that of the second-grade skills tests, and to clearly define the content of these skills and the process of acquiring them.

In addition to the public exams for the 133 listed skills, official recognition is also awarded to "in-company tests," a system whereby the employer or an industry organization tests workers in their own firm or industry, subject to authorization under standards set by the Ministry of Labor.

Initially, intermediate skills could perhaps be tested along the lines of this in-company testing system. But if the basic intermediate skills are to gain wide recognition by employers, the foreign workers themselves, and society in general, the scope of the official testing system will have to be extended to cover at least five hundred skills.

Encouraging Employers to Adopt Intermediate Skills CDPs

Employers wanting to employ foreign workers, and particularly those who wish to participate in the kind of work-and-learn program I have advocated, must be persuaded to adopt intermediate-skills CDPs on as wide a scale as possible.

Before this can be done, however, the government and the private sector must cooperate in developing such programs. Employers taking on foreign trainees must then be obliged to implement the programs, and some kind of system set up to make absolutely sure that they do so.

The system must be properly enforced because, unless employers take responsibility for implementing CDPs, there is a real danger workers will end up being made to do manual labor and fail to receive any training at all. After all, as far as employers are concerned, the main attraction of foreign workers is that they will do, without complaint, the kind of unskilled manual jobs that Japanese workers refuse to do. Meanwhile there is no shortage of Japanese workers willing to do jobs that demand skills and training. If left to their own devices, many employers will undoubtedly take on unskilled foreigners to do the "dirty, demanding, and dangerous" manual jobs that Japanese workers shy away from.

It will not be easy to force such employers to implement CDPs. The more demanding the skills, the more it costs employers, and the less it benefits them, to conduct training programs. There are plenty of Japanese willing to do jobs that demand these relatively higher-level skills, and training foreigners—given the communication difficulties and differences in customs—is bound to incur all sorts of extra costs. But using foreigners only for unskilled manual work and then packing them off home again will lay Japan open to charges of exploitation— of using foreign labor only where it is profitable, treating it as a throwaway commodity. So employers must be made to implement career development programs even if it involves a certain amount of cost outlay.

The first priority, then, is for the government and private sector to jointly develop career development programs for intermediate skills.

Joint Government/Private-Sector CDP Manuals

The main function of CDPs for intermediate skills will be to provide practical guidelines and standards for employers, particularly small-business employers, seeking to impart skills to foreign workers.

Work-and-learn employment differs from ordinary employment in that its primary object is training. At the same time as they are working, trainees are learning skills that will be of some practical use when they return to their home countries. It cannot be called a work-and-learn program unless foreign workers learn skills and receive training.

Employers, however, although they may understand the aims of the program in principle, are faced with a number of basic problems. They are often unsure about what specific skills they should teach trainees, what kind of training and practical work experience they are supposed to offer, and whether their premises are properly equipped to provide training. If they go to the city government office for advice, they are told to work these things out for themselves. Large corporations with sophisticated management skills and experts who can be mobilized to help in training are of course able to work out training programs on their own, but most small companies cannot.

First of all, small-business employers have not the vaguest idea what sorts of skills are likely to prove useful when foreign workers return home. Most small-business proprietors are well-intentioned and conscientious, so they do their best to impart the skills that are valued most highly in their own businesses. But these skills may not necessarily be of much use to trainees. There is also a great deal of variation in the ways different employers manage their businesses, the types of skills that they use, their attitudes to skills, and their levels of understanding of the skill formation process. Hence firms and employers are bound to differ greatly in terms of the way they actually conduct training.

If the nature of work-and-learn employment differed this widely among different firms and employers, the trainees themselves would have difficulty understanding what was meant by the concept, and the government would find it very hard both to administer the system and to measure its effectiveness. A skill formation program would hardly be worthy of the name if some employers made conscientious efforts to impart skills while others showed very little interest. Such a program would very quickly degenerate into a pretext for exploiting foreign workers as a source of low-wage manual labor.

If such damaging consequences are to be avoided, then, the first priority is to draft guidelines for employers, setting out in clear terms the types of training and work experience, and how much of it, they must offer trainees for each separate type of skill.

Initially, guidelines could perhaps be drawn up for about 500 skills, and the range eventually extended to cover one or two thousand. But government offices can hardly be expected to have access to practical information on such a wide range of skills. At first, therefore, they and other work-and-learn employment organizations would have to compile this information with the help of private-sector organizations in each of the industries in question.

For most intermediate skills, as we have seen, this kind of information is not available because it has never been codified or written down. Industry organizations will have to start, therefore, by analyzing the situation in their own industries, with the help of experts in each field. As they gather and analyze the data, the government side will have to supply concepts, an analytical framework, and standards for evaluation.

If government and industry cooperate in this way, it should not be too difficult to produce guidelines for the formation of some 500 intermediate skills. All industries and professions have their own representative organizations, and in any case intermediate skills are actually being learned in industry all the time. All that is needed is for the relevant government offices and agencies to give industry organizations a deadline—say six months—within which to gather the data on skills for their own industry. After all the materials have been submitted, a team made up of government officials, private-sector representatives, and some independent experts can then sit down and examine the data more closely before editing them into the form of manuals.

For the sake of clarity and convenience, the completed manuals for each carefully defined industry and skill should be made up of three sections which (1) define the exact nature of the intermediate skill and what level of competence signifies its mastery, (2) contain flow-charts detailing each stage of training and work experience in the process of acquiring skills, and (3) contain a clear and simple definition of the content of each skill.

Manuals could then be distributed to all employers wishing to take on work-and-learn trainees. Employers would be expected to fully understand their own manual and set up programs that closely follow its guidelines. Manuals would have to be brief and well edited so that employers could easily refer to them at any time. They should give concrete examples of the tasks involved in each skill, and include clear one-page flow-charts summarizing the process of formation of the skill, which could be detached from the manual and displayed at the workplace.

A Social Enforcement System to Guarantee the Formation of Intermediate Skills

Let us now turn to the government's second policy task—that of enforcing the implementation of skill formation programs. As I have said, one of the chief merits of foreign workers from the employer's point of view is that they will readily do certain types of work that Japanese workers will not do. Training foreign workers to do more complex work that involves learning intermediate skills increases employers' cost burden due to the time and trouble involved. Honest and well-disposed employers may still make an effort to ensure that trainees acquire skills in line with the aims of the program. But others will undoubtedly try to avoid the cost and effort of imparting skills unless there is some system to monitor them effectively.

Since skill formation is part of an employer's business activity and basically a matter of individual discretion, one obviously wants to avoid having to enforce it by law. And even if legal sanctions were employed, it would be very difficult in practice to guarantee that every employer complied with the law.

As an alternative to legal enforcement, I have for some time advocated using the network of Japanese society. The idea would be to use the mesh of mutual supervision that already exists within industry and professional organizations, particularly at the local level.

Japanese industry is very intricately organized, with regional chambers of commerce, commerce associations in every town and village, small and medium-sized business organizations in every industry, and professional and vocational organizations for every profession. These organizations could be put to use to ensure that employers played by the rules.

Large and middle-ranking corporations with overseas offices will be able to participate in work-and-learn programs on their own. But most medium and small businesses, lacking the resources of large corporations, will have to form groups under the auspices of local industry organizations which will act as nominal sponsors.

Since smaller businesses can only participate in this way, the group as a whole could be held accountable and forfeit its right to take part in the program if any of its members was perceived to have neglected its commitment to intermediate skill formation. The just would suffer for the sins of the unjust. Past experience shows that this kind of social coercion tends to work in Japanese society.

While the idea of group responsibility is somewhat anachronistic, and I personally find it distasteful, nevertheless Japan's treatment of foreign workers is a subtle, sensitive, and important human issue that matters greatly to the future of the nation and its international relations, and differs qualitatively from ordinary economic problems. The world will not allow Japan to indulge in any further discrimination, abuse, or exploitation of foreign workers. It is essential to attain the work-and-learn program's objective of forming intermediate skills even if this means resorting to such a system of social enforcement by means of a "neighborhood association" style of mutual monitoring.

Effectiveness of CDPs for Intermediate Skills

The spread and full implementation of intermediate skills CDPs in workplaces throughout the nation will have beneficial effects in a number of different areas. Let us take a look at the main benefits we can predict.

First, they will have an educational effect in establishing standards for skill formation. Most proprietors of small businesses taking on foreign workers or work-and-learn trainees, while they may be sincerely committed to skill formation, have neither the time nor the knowledge to devise systematic training and work experience programs. CDPs would therefore serve as handy and effective guidelines for such employers. In addition, they would definitely serve to lessen the temptation of employers to use foreign workers for manual labor.

Second, CDPs will provide an effective means of testing the level of skills foreign trainees have acquired. They will make it easier to institute skills tests, since the content of the intermediate skills in each industry and the type of job will be clearly defined. Separate skills tests should be conducted in each industry and job-type, and trainees awarded certificates of proficiency.

The skill formation and testing system should go some way toward giving foreign workers and trainees a definite objective and a career plan, as well as a sense of pride and confidence.

Another beneficial effect of CDPs is that increased awareness of intermediate skills throughout industry, and the introduction of clear standards for their formation, will give a powerful boost to overseas direct investment by companies involved in the work-and-learn program. The business activity of small firms, like that of large corporations, is going to have to become increasingly globalized. Companies will be forced overseas by Japan's high cost of living and high domestic wage costs. For Japanese firms making direct investments in the Asian region, a reservoir of Asian workers possessing intermediate skills which they acquired in Japan, and which are widely acknowledged by Japanese industry, will represent an extremely valuable intangible resource.

CDPs will also benefit Japan's future workforce by acting as a template for the creation of human resources. As Japan's economic structure changes and its workforce diversifies, the labor market is rapidly moving away from the traditional dual structure of a lifetime employment sector and a marginal (temporary and part-time workers) sector, toward a new structure that interposes a highly mobile intermediate labor market between the traditional inner and outer markets. Under this new structure, there will be an increasing need to define marketable intermediate skills. A system that clearly sets out the process of acquiring these skills, and introduces definite standards and qualifications, will restore pride and confidence to the more mobile sectors of the workforce—young people, women, and the elderly— and will be of great benefit in fostering a healthy attitude toward work in Japanese society.

2. Concrete Examples of Intermediate Skills

So far in this chapter we have discussed the concept and significance of intermediate skills in rather general terms, but I would now like to look at some concrete examples of intermediate skills in industry and consider the potential opportunities they present. We will look at a number of examples from various different industries, which should give us a clearer idea of what exactly intermediate skills are, and what specifically needs to done to create the conditions for the acquisition of these skills by foreign workers.

Engineering

The engineering industry is primarily concerned with the design and installation of equipment, in factories for example. Engineering work involves rather complex operations such as pipe-laying, with the result that it can be divided into a large number of basic skilled jobs. These include plumbing, canning, electric welding, fitting, and instrumentation.

Over the past few years, company A has built up a solid record of training foreigners in intermediate engineering skills. With reference to company A's experience, then, let us review the situation in the industry and survey the potential for foreign trainees to form intermediate engineering skills.

Company A is a mid-ranking firm involved in the construction of petrochemical and oil-refining plants all over the world. Recently it has helped construct plants in Saudi Arabia, Iran, Iraq, Kuwait, Singapore, and Algeria. In its overseas construction projects the firm has employed not only Japanese engineers and skilled workers but also skilled workers from third countries like the Philippines, China, Malaysia, and Thailand, who were trained by the company in-house and employed on overseas projects as assistants.

Company A runs systematic training programs for overseas workers, based on a long-term plan. A total of some 500 Filipino trainees have participated in five successive training programs over the last six years, each lasting one year.

The first week of the training course is spent in orientation. Trainees are given an introductory grounding in the purpose of the course, Japanese law and customs, and elementary Japanese language. This is followed by a three-day introduction to the workplace coupled with general guidance for living in Japan and instruction in health and safety, work regulations, and dormitory rules.

For the following year trainees study and train on-the-job at the same time. The study element consists of 10 hours of Japanese language instruction and 32 hours of technical lectures per month, conducted at the company's training center. On-the-job-training in various skills is carried out at the company's plants. The main skills are canning, pipe-laying, electric welding, design engineering, fitting, and instrumentation.

Trainees in canning start out with cutting, then learn the bending process before practicing the whole operation. At the same time they study elementary, and then intermediate-level, interpretation of diagrams.

Pipe-laying trainees begin with cutting and temporary fitting, then progress to harnessing, fitting and fixing, on-site gas pipe welding, secondary assembly, heat-bending, and pipe fitting, with some of the skills being learned in parallel.

Electric welding trainees spend the first few months intensively practicing on-site welding of gas pipes, to give them familiarity with welding in various directions. Then they move on to high-pressure welding, SUS welding, arc-welding, and x-ray analysis.

Design engineering trainees start off interpreting and drawing pipe layout diagrams, then move on to practical training in the various design skills and in materials classification.

Trainees in fitting study machine-work and blueprint interpretation, in parallel with practical skills like hardening and annealing, machine installation, equipment maintenance, measurement, and inspection.

The course in instrumentation also starts with blueprint reading and development. At the same time trainees study pipe-laying, wiring, materials, care of tools, electric theory, instrument assembly, measurement, and inspection.

Ideally these courses would equip trainees with a sufficiently versatile set of skills to handle any of a variety of jobs, but this takes quite a few years even for Japanese employees. Nevertheless company A does hold out this objective. All trainees except those studying design engineering are examined for the JIS welding certificate, and so far nearly all have passed. Since company A is a MITI-approved examiner, trainees can be tested on the company premises. Welding is the only skill in which they can obtain a qualification within the one-year training period, but they can build up their skills in other fields through on-the-job training (OJT).

Electric welding plays a major role in plant construction and is one of the most basic engineering skills. Trainees who have learned basic welding skills through intensive training on a construction site can generally start working as welders after one to two years. But mastering intermediate skills generally takes two to three years. Intermediate engineering skills would be, for example, sheathed arc welding and TIG welding from all body positions. These skills are universally applicable and enable workers to cope with 60% to 80% of the welding work on most construction sites.

More training is required for specialized work like nuclear-related construction and the handling of special alloys. These skills are said to take an additional ten years to master, though this depends on the individual.

OJT is an indispensable part of the training process, not only for welding but for all construction-site skills. Company A has found that the most effective way to give trainees OJT is to send them to work at the construction sites of affiliated domestic firms after they have completed their formal training at the company's training center.

The knowledge that trainees have accumulated during the study period of training comes to life when they put it into practice on the construction site. Only when they actually start working on site do trainees come to appreciate the meaning of the safety and other regulations, and the differences between blueprints and the real thing. On-site training has many other merits as well. Trainees become aware of the importance of quality control, learn efficient work procedures and the value of teamwork, and come to understand the whole work process and the position of their own job within it.

After finishing these training courses combined with practical on-site training, trainees go on to build up practical experience on overseas sites. Some are later recalled to Japan for retraining to upgrade their skills.

Company A has found through experience that a number of problems can arise in training foreign workers in intermediate skills. First, the one-year training period is too short. As we saw in the example of electric welding, it takes Japanese workers two or three years just to master the lowest-level intermediate skills in this field, and foreigners are likely to take longer because of the language barrier. It is important, therefore, for the company to instill a sense of optimism in trainees by offering talented individuals the opportunity to continue working for the company as employees after they have completed their training.

Company A has also experienced difficulties with OJT. Although OJT largely determines the success or failure of training programs as a whole, company A has encountered a number of obstacles in trying to implement OJT programs, due to a lack of understanding by some of the government agencies concerned with training. Government agencies must recognize OJT as the foundation of training, acknowledge that there is a work element in practical training programs, and allow appropriate remuneration for the work trainees do, so as to give them some sense of job satisfaction.

Another problem is that, since the written part of the official skills tests is in Japanese, it is extremely difficult for foreign trainees to pass tests and obtain qualifications, no matter how competent they may be in terms of practical ability. In both company and public examinations it should be permissible to translate questions into English or the trainees' native languages. This would create an environment in which it is easier for foreign candidates to be tested and obtain skills qualifications.

Finally, customers for engineering services are still reluctant to take on foreign trainees, and there are very few in-service training opportunities for higher-level skills like construction or management techniques. More employers should open the doors wider to trainees and contribute much more to raising the level of skills and techniques in the countries they come from.

Automobile Manufacture

Automobile manufacturing is a complex and widely diffused industry. Twenty thousand parts have to be collected and assembled to manufacture a single passenger car. Hence the final assembly stage of the process is supported by a multilayered structure of subcontracting parts manufacturers.

There is a wide range of parts manufacturers, all supplying different types of parts destined for different stages of the manufacturing process. Manufacturers of simple parts usually depend on a rather limited number of skills such as metal processing. This is true not only in the automobile industry but also of most small-scale manufacturers in the machine metal processing field. Auto makers, on the other hand, have to assemble enormous numbers of different parts on production lines in an orderly and efficient manner, so they have to be much larger and more complex. The work requires a large number of different skills of various levels.

Let us now consider the potential for foreign workers to acquire intermediate skills in the automobile industry, by referring to the case of company B, a major automobile manufacturer.

Company B is a multinational company with a worldwide sales network and manufacturing and assembly bases all over the world. Obviously companies of this scale need to train foreign employees if they are to conduct sales, customer service, and manufacturing activities smoothly. Aside from its own employees, however, company B also accepts foreign trainees under an international technical cooperation program. It refers to its training activities in general as "overseas training."

The company runs four different kinds of overseas training programs, directed at (1) manufacturing and assembly plant staff (manufacturing, service, parts), (2) distribution staff (service, parts), (3) major users (service, parts), and (4) international technical cooperation trainees (service, manufacturing). The content of training can be broadly divided into (1) manufacturing (production and quality control, manufacturing technology), (2) service (service plant management, service technology), and (3) parts (parts sales, stock control), and the main object of the program is to train "key persons" in these fields.

The automobiles company B manufactures, whether in Japan or at overseas production bases, first pass through the hands of overseas distributors, and are then supplied to a large network of dealers before finally being delivered to customers. And since cars are consumer products, they require maintenance and other forms of servicing. To make sure all this production activity, servicing, and parts management goes smoothly, the company must constantly improve its performance through the education and training of overseas staff. This is the basic task of the overseas training program.

The company's overseas production bases and distributors run training courses on a continuous basis, and the head office dispatches staff to conduct special on-site courses as the need arises. This can be convenient when overseas plants have to train large numbers of people at one time. The company also invites staff from overseas sales offices to the head office training center for regular intensive courses when necessary.

Nearly all the work carried out at company B's various work sites demands some intermediate-level skills. However, since automobile manufacturers conform to the typical pattern of an "internalized" labor market made up of a combination of many different types of job, workers tend to absorb intermediate skills automatically through the internal training process, as they rise through the ranks of the organization. Few of these skills are recognized as having any currency of their own.

Workers at an auto manufacturer must learn a number of intermediate-level skills in order to carry out their jobs responsibly. But acquiring skills is no more than one step in a much longer and more wide-ranging career process that includes promotion and various changes of job. Foreign employees working in such an "inner market" are in the same boat, insofar as they follow the usual route to promotion and build up careers in the organization.

While it makes sense to identify and describe these intermediate skills as career steps in clarifying models of different job-types, the skills have meaning only within the context of career formation under the lifetime employment system.

Company B also cooperates in the Central Human Resources Development Council's Overseas Youth Skills Training Program, as a philanthropic contribution, and conducts training courses for young people from the developing countries at its overseas training center. In 1990–91 it invited trainees from Thailand, Malaysia, and Indonesia to attend a 21-month training course. The course was made up of the following main elements:

Months 1–3: Introductory training—Japanese language and guidance for everyday life in Japan.

Months 4–6: Basic skills training—assembly, paintwork, welding processes, basic engineering (lectures), handling machines, and quality checking (practical).

Months 7–21: On-the-job training—assembly, paintwork, welding processes, site management, quality control, machinery maintenance, small group activities, and assembly-line work.

Trainees pick up a certain amount of knowledge and experience in such training courses, but most automobile production processes in Japan today are fully automated; robots are used extensively, and the technology is extremely advanced. Hence one cannot be optimistic that such training will give trainees anything like all the knowledge and skills they will need to work in car production in their home countries. There still seems to be a significant gap between the content of the training and the actual needs of developing countries.

Metal Processing

Metal processing is one of the basic industries that shores up the manufacturing sector. It is made up of a vast number of small and medium-sized firms that mostly act as subcontractors for machinery and metal products manufacturers. Most of these firms are at present suffering from a severe shortage of skilled labor.

Company C is a small town-based factory, with only 20 employees, which processes precision-tooled metal parts for watches and cameras. Its main business is cutting to size metal bars and steel plates already processed by another factory. It machine-processes these materials into finished products using lathes, tabletop metal cutters, and pattern adjusters, and then tests the products using measuring equipment such as dial gauges and projectors.

It takes about three years to master all these skills. Workers have to fully understand how the various machines work, learn to handle and adjust them, and develop the skills to manufacture products to a high degree of precision.

Company C employs a small number of foreign workers, who work hard and pay their own way. But their motive for working appears to be confined to the wages they earn, and does not extend to learning new skills. Even if they do learn some skills, it is rather doubtful that similar firms in their home countries would be in a position to use the extremely sophisticated and complex machinery that these workers are learning to operate in Japan.

Bookbinding

The bookbinding industry is made up of some 1,500 small firms nationwide, with a combined annual turnover of 5 trillion yen. Nearly all of these firms specialize in a specific field. Broadly, the industry can be divided into (1) top-grade binding (hardbacks and fancy bindings), (2) ordinary-grade binding (paperbacks), (3) magazines, (4) pocket diaries, (5) ledgers and notebooks, and (6) library bindings; each of these sectors demands slightly different skills.

The industry was extremely labor-intensive until about twenty years ago, but today, with increasing mechanization and technical advances in binding adhesives, most of the former skills of the trade are no longer of any use, and there is an urgent need for a new infusion of skilled labor. In addition, since the industry relies on orders from publishers, many bookbinding firms are subcontractors and have to bear the brunt of price fluctuations.

There is a serious labor shortage; young people are unwilling to continue family businesses, and the future of the industry as a whole looks bleak.

The basic process of high-grade bookbinding involves a number of steps. First the paper has to be trued up, then cut to size; the pages have to be folded, glued, and arranged in order; the backs have to be stitched and pressed to prevent unevenness; and glue has to be applied to the spine and dried. After a final cut, the spine must be rounded out and sewn; the already-prepared cover is fitted and joined to the book, and then the finished book is finally pressed once more.

The bookbinding industry now uses separate machines for the first half of the process (cutting, folding, gluing and stitching), and the leading firms have considerably shortened it, though it is not yet completely mechanized. Meanwhile the second half of the process has been totally mechanized, and anyone can now cope with the job if they just learn how to operate the machinery. The first half still requires deft fingerwork, and many techniques still require a certain knack. For example, the machines have to be put on a different setting for each book, and the paper also behaves differently depending on the season. Experience is valuable, and some veterans of the industry claim to be able to make all the necessary adjustments simply "by ear," instinctively.

Company D is a mid-ranking firm in the industry, operating seven machines and employing seven people. Employees first learn how to sheave the paper, then how to stack it and line up the corners. After some time they are taught what to do if things go wrong, and how to adjust the machines. After three years working at company D, one Pakistani employee is now adept at fine-tuning the machines.

There are full-time training courses for bookbinders, for example at specialist institutions like the Tokyo College of Bookbinding Skills, which runs a systematic one-year program offering practical training in all the bookbinding processes and courses in introductory bookbinding, bookbinding methods and machinery, production engineering, electrical engineering, and health and safety.

After completing a one-year course at such a college and gaining a year's further experience, bookbinding students qualify for Grade 2 of the state examination in bookbinding skills. But the skills they learn in college really only qualify them to bind books by hand. There is quite a gap between these skills and those used in the industry, which is now considerably mechanized. To really master the craft, therefore, students have to learn not only hand-binding skills but also the techniques of machinery operation.

A combination of a year's study at a bookbinding college with a year's OJT, learning how to operate the machinery, would probably constitute a good program for foreign trainees. Not only would they be able to experience the whole field, from the basics of bookbinding to the most up-to-date techniques, but they could probably put the hand-binding techniques to good use when they returned home, and could also start businesses if they learned some basic cost accounting and bookkeeping skills as well.

Construction

Due to the working conditions on construction sites, employer-worker relations, and the fact that demand is easily influenced by fluctuations in the economy, construction site workers tend to be highly mobile, and the construction industry tends to suffer from severe labor shortages at times when the economy is doing well and business is booming.

In addition, the Japanese workforce is aging along with the population as a whole, and younger Japanese brought up in an age of affluence tend to shy away from unpleasant and menial jobs. Hence the industry faces a severe shortage of younger workers.

In an industry with such a cyclical and structural shortage of labor, one can well surmise that there is a rapidly growing latent demand for foreign labor. The large numbers of unskilled foreigners now working illegally on Japanese construction sites have indeed been drawn in by this demand.

While building and construction is a huge industry that employs around six million people nationwide, it has a complex multilayered structure, with a small number of very large general construction companies at the apex and innumerable small family-run businesses beneath. The great majority of the illegal foreign workers are thought to have been absorbed by the small businesses and family-run contractors positioned at the end of the chain of subcontractors, though the real situation is far from clear.

The construction industry draws together an array of advanced techniques for building a wide variety of structures under diverse environmental conditions. Builders have to work with great precision and stick closely to plans, and the process requires the coordinated mobilization of many high-level skills and techniques.

For example, a public-works project might require scaffolders, stone masons, block-layers, electricians, reinforced concrete workers, painters, welders, caisson workers, tunnel specialists, bridge specialists, rail track workers, molding box makers, carpenters, plasterers, plumbers, waterproofing specialists, sheet-metal workers, tilers, aluminum window fitters, roofers, glaziers, interior finishers, carpenters, ventilation duct workers, insulation workers, and equipment and machinery fitters. If foreign labor could be introduced for skilled jobs like these, most of the social and economic problems we have noted could probably be resolved or avoided.

Skills almost identical to those practiced in Japan are in demand to some extent in construction industries all over the world. But different countries all have their own particular standards, work practices, and methods of teaching and utilizing skills. Hence it is not necessarily easy to transfer the skills used in country A to country B without some modification.

First there is the language problem. Language differences can be a much greater obstacle than is often realized when it comes to skills training and to testing trainees for proficiency. Then there is the question of skills accreditation. What level of education, experience, and mastery of a given skill amounts to competence in that skill? Every country has its own education, training, and qualification systems. The question is how to establish common standards among them.

Finally, there is the problem of actual work practices. The reading of plans, drawing up of contracts, methods of measurement, and management of subcontracted work all vary from one construction site to another, and working methods often cannot be adapted to fit a uniform system of training.

In view of these practical problems, we can infer that a skills training program for foreign workers will require a considerable amount of careful organization if it is to achieve its objectives. It must properly evaluate, foster, and utilize the abilities that workers bring with them from countries with strikingly different conditions to those in Japan. This will involve a great deal of work in developing and organizing suitable educational and training programs, Japanese language courses, and accreditation tests that are easier for foreign workers to take. But these tasks are by no means impossible.

It usually takes workers three to five years to master the construction industry skills listed above to a level where they can be safely left in charge of work on a construction site. I have called such skills "intermediate skills" but most of them correspond to the level of Grade 2 of the official Japanese skills testing system.

There is now a need to conduct a careful review of the intermediate skills used in each type of job—to recognize them, assess the relative standards for these skills in the foreign workers' countries, and develop proper curricula, work-and-learn programs, and skills tests more suited to people from diverse backgrounds.

The Construction Industry Education Center Foundation, founded in 1991, has made significant advances in this direction. The foundation's aim is to train skilled construction industry workers in the developing countries as a foreign-aid contribution. It deserves credit for its efforts to promote Japanese language education and on-the-job training.

Food-Services Industry

"Food services" is a general term covering the various services offered by the catering industry, which is made up of a wide range of establishments from major chain stores to small family-run bars and restaurants. It is a large and steadily growing industry, with a total annual turnover of 24 trillion yen in 1990.

As a service industry, it employs large numbers of people, but there is a high level of labor mobility, and the industry is now facing a chronic and structural shortage of workers. Consequently there is a significant latent demand for foreign labor.

The industry includes many different types of business, but here let us look at the potential for intermediate skill formation by foreign workers in one of the largest and most modern sectors of the industry, that of chain-store restaurants.

Although most chain-store restaurants are facing a labor shortage and the latent demand for foreign labor is quite strong, very few of them have yet employed foreigners or taken on foreign trainees, due to the legal difficulties involved, the absence of any proper skills formation programs, and the lack of any commonly acknowledged standards. Given some improvement in these areas, however, there is considerable scope for expanding training, OJT, and employment opportunities for foreigners, centered on intermediate skills. Let us now consider the possibilities, with reference to the experience of one fast-food chain.

Company E is one of the larger restaurant chains, employing some 30,000 people in restaurants throughout the country, some of which are under direct management. On average, each store employs three full-time workers plus 40 to 50 part-timers, who work, on average, four-hour shifts. The company employs 20 Chinese and Bangladeshi foreigners nationwide, but they work mainly in the kitchens, and only for up to 20 hours a week. Several other major and mid-ranking firms in the industry employ similar numbers of foreign workers.

Part-time foreign workers tend to be university or Japanese language students, and are not in a position to form skills in any real sense, given the limited number of hours they are permitted to work under the current Immigration Law. They are simply doing manual labor on a piecework basis.

Company E is now planning a major expansion into Southeast Asia, which will require very close cooperation on staff training between the Japanese catering industry and that in the Asian countries from which workers come to Japan. The government should recognize the need for such cooperation and take steps to facilitate it. The present law binds employers hand and foot, making it impossible to take on foreign labor with any peace of mind. Company E feels that the government should legislate to clarify working hours and conditions of employment for foreigners, and that the industry should make stronger efforts to allocate workers. Company E would then be able to accept foreign workers without guilt or fear of arousing suspicion, and could invest management resources in the Asian countries with their enormous latent potential for business growth.

Clearly there is a range of intermediate-level skills in the catering industry that foreign workers could be taught and safely left to apply unattended. At present, however, as company E's experience shows, Japan does not have the legal or institutional infrastructure for firms to train unskilled foreigners in these skills, and thereby invest in human resources, without sacrificing profitability. Hence the industry employs only a very small number of foreigners at present, and they are mostly assigned to manual and cleaning work in the kitchens. No progress has yet been made towards establishing a systematic skill formation program for foreign workers.

Many of the larger and mid-ranking firms in the catering industry, such as the "family restaurants," which are highly systematized chain-store organizations, have rationalized their business to a very high degree, introduced staff manuals, and established their own CDPs covering the full range of skills from basic restaurant work through management. These CDPs generally incorporate the following steps.

(1) Restaurant Workers: simple cooking skills (basically heating pre-frozen foods), customer service (taking orders, delivering orders to the kitchen, bringing orders to the tables, and working the cash register), general duties (washing up, cleaning, etc.). These jobs are nearly all filled by part-time and temporary staff.

(2) Assistant Shop-Manager: has knowledge of all restaurant work, and plays a central role in the operation of the restaurant.

(3) Shop Manager, Head of Sales Office: overall charge of restaurant, supervision of restaurant workers, client administration, management and training of subordinate staff.

(4) Head Office Staff: responsible for an area or several sales offices. Making up menus, price management, purchasing management, sales planning and promotion, and data management.

(5) Head Office Management Executives: drawing up and planning of company policy, staff training and supervision, and other management duties.

Company F, a major firm in the meals-supply industry, has given bird names—duck, pigeon, swallow, falcon, hawk, eagle—to the various steps in its career development program. At company G, a major Japanese-style chain restaurant, employees do restaurant work, corresponding to (1) above, for their first one to two years in the firm, move on to stage (2) from their third year, move up to stage (3) from around their fifth year, and after ten years' experience are promoted to the position of area manager or head office supervisor. Company E says that in the early days after it was established, employees were made shop managers (stage 3) after only six months, but ideally employees should spend about 8 years doing all the various jobs in rotation before moving on to work at head office in product development or planning. As an incentive to longer-serving members of staff, the company's CDP allows them to set up on their own under an employee-franchise arrangement.

From the above survey we can draw several conclusions regarding the formation of intermediate skills by foreign workers in the catering industry.

First of all, while the industry faces a chronic labor shortage and there is strong latent demand for foreign labor, present legislation discourages firms from investing in skills training. Hence only a very small number of unskilled foreign workers are employed in the industry as yet, and most of them are part-timers assigned to general kitchen duties. Some firms do train foreigners as a development aid contribution, but such training activities are generally loss-producing.

Meanwhile, the highly organized chain-restaurant businesses have systematic career development programs which could easily be adapted to foreign workers, given the necessary changes in the law. Foreigners could then be trained in any of the intermediate skills, as restaurant workers, shop managers, sales office assistant managers, or even head office staff.

The catering industry is now entering an era of global expansion, and it makes good strategic sense at this point to train foreigners and build up human capital. An industry-wide effort to institute Japanese language training programs and multilingual training manuals would, subject to an improvement in the legal position of foreign workers, make it significantly easier for them to acquire intermediate skills and also help create useful human capital, not only for Japan but for other countries as well.

Linen Supply

The linen supply business involves the laundering of linen products and the renting out and collecting of such products on a continuous basis. It includes cleaning firms, but not ordinary dry-cleaners that cater directly to the public. The cleaning and leasing sides of the industry interlock with each other. The main clients are hotels and restaurants, and the industry as a whole continues to expand, comprising some 4,000 businesses nationwide and employing about 60,000 people. The majority are small businesses with from 10 to 20 employees.

According to one survey, nearly 60% of the relatively large suppliers that belong to the Linen Supply Association have at some time employed foreign workers, and 40% currently employ foreigners. Each of these firms employs anywhere from two or three to more than twenty foreigners, most of whom do manual jobs like sorting laundry.

Company H is one of the largest firms in the industry, with over 550 employees. It employs a small number of Chinese, Bangladeshis, and Vietnamese. The company houses them in private rented accommodation at company expense and employs them to do simple tasks like sorting.

The company employs large numbers of part-time and temporary workers to do such manual jobs, which are labor-intensive because they are resistant to mechanization. There is therefore a strong latent demand for foreign labor to fill this need. Other jobs, however, like laundering, drying, and distribution, are becoming increasingly mechanized, and there are now a number of jobs that demand higher-level skills, such as machine operation, waste-water disposal, machine maintenance, and computer control. Company H has appointed a Chinese employee with computer skills to a stock control position, with apparently satisfactory results.

Haulage

The haulage industry is a wide-ranging and key industry covering many different kinds of distribution. But the road-haulage sector, which is the mainstay of the industry, faces compound difficulties. Road-haulage has been linked to worsening environmental problems like road congestion and the air pollution from truck exhaust. Working conditions for employees have been slow to improve, and the industry faces an increasingly severe shortage of labor.

Some sectors of the industry have shown interest in using foreign labor, but the majority view is that other urgent matters should be tackled first: modernization and rationalization of the industry, improving working conditions, and minimizing damage to the environment. And while the shortage of truck drivers has become a chronic problem, there are difficulties in employing foreign workers as drivers, due to the labor laws and to language problems. Distribution is, after all, a service industry, and language could prove a significant barrier. Foreigners might be able to work loading and unloading trucks, but working as a member of a trucking crew involves not only knowing one's own specialized job but having a good grasp of the business as a whole. If the various specialist tasks were mechanized and computerized, it would probably be possible to introduce foreign labor, at least in jobs that basically involve delivery.

Company I is one of the larger firms in the industry. It has not yet hired any foreign workers, but is teaching skills to a trainee from the city transport office in Tianjin, China. If the company seeks to expand overseas in the future, this kind of training will probably come to assume much greater significance.

Medical Treatment and Welfare Work

The Japanese population is now rapidly aging, and there are fears of a shortage of workers for medical treatment and welfare work. In 1988 this sector employed 2.2 million people, but the Ministry of Health and Welfare estimates it will need to employ at least 3.46 million by the year 2000. The main reason is the great expansion in demand that is forecast for workers at homes for the elderly.

Securing enough medical and welfare workers to meet this kind of increase in demand in just a few years will be no easy task. Meanwhile the sector is studying the possibility of switching from the facility-based pattern of care that has predominated up to now to a more home-treatment-oriented approach. Due also to the labor shortage and cutbacks in equipment investment, it now seems inevitable that we will see an increase in the relative importance of home-treatment types of medical and welfare services.

As this happens, there is bound to be a great increase in demand for home helpers to assist in caring for people at home. Some excellent research by Eiko Shinozuka, based on a questionnaire survey of Brazilian women of Japanese descent working as home helpers (80% of whom were trained as practical nurses in hospitals), has examined the possibility of introducing foreign labor for home-based medical treatment and welfare work.[1] Shinozuka cites several conditions for the useful participation of foreign workers in this type of work: (1) that workers possess a certain amount of Japanese language ability, (2) that home-care skills are specialized and improved, (3) that workers are guaranteed accommodation in Japan, and (4) that the old-fashioned housekeeper placement agencies are reformed.

The Health and Welfare Ministry has instituted qualifications for "welfare carers," in an effort to raise the professional status of these jobs, and the Ministry of Labor has introduced a similar accreditation system for "care attendants," based on practical experience, since most people who have worked as housekeepers have had some experience in home-help situations. While there may be problems in having two mutually exclusive qualifications sanctioned by two separate ministries, it is important that society acknowledges care work as a specialist intermediate skill and that no time is lost in giving foreign workers access to the acquisition of this skill.

Responding to Latent Needs and Realizing Potential
Much can be learned from the situations in the various industries and skills formation processes we have surveyed above.

First, there is an extremely significant latent need for the formation of intermediate skills by foreign workers. There is, potentially at least, a considerable need for foreign workers to do skilled jobs in a wide range of industries from engineering, automobile manufacture, metal processing, and construction to bookbinding, food services, linen supply, medical treatment, and welfare. Engineering Company A provides us with a pioneering example of a firm which has taken practical steps to train foreign workers in intermediate skills vitally important to the industry. As I have stressed, forming intermediate skills not only benefits the foreign workers themselves but also helps Japanese industry and society, as well as the economies of the sender countries.

Second, the case studies show that intermediate skills are in fact real, substantial skills. I have described them as skills that enable a worker to be safely left in charge of the running of a workplace. These skills are fundamental to all industries and types of job. One could say, conversely, that unless workers master these skills they cannot safely be left to work unattended.

The problem is that since these skills tend to be learned automatically in the course of people's work experience, their content is hardly ever explicitly defined in writing or in manual form. Workers pick them up through a process of tacit understanding, and they tend to go unrecognized and unappreciated by the community at large. While it is clear that these intermediate skills do exist in all the various industries and job-types we have surveyed, they still need to be clearly defined to give them universal recognition. Since they are real and substantial skills, it should be perfectly possible to describe them and come up with concrete programs for their formation.

Third, implementing intermediate skills programs requires not only recognizing the significance of the skills but also resolving to reform the present systems that prevent training programs from being implemented.

Fourth, a basis must be established for intermediate skills programs. The most appropriate length for training courses, preferably involving on-the-job training, should be determined. We can infer from the situation in the industries we surveyed that the optimum training period will probably be from two to five years.

Fifth, although foreign workers will be primarily engaged in training, they will also be working during the period they are gaining work experience. The legal system should take account of this and recognize their position as workers, so that they can be paid a wage appropriate to the work they do and be properly protected as employees; this will in turn motivate them to put their experience to best use.

Sixth, if intermediate skills are to become widely recognized in society and skills programs are to become widely used in workplaces, it is vital that the government and the private sector work together to collect information, analyze the situation, draft standards, assist in the organization of programs, and create the institutional conditions for the skills to be recognized and tested.

Note

[1] Eiko Shinozuka, "Brazilian-Japanese Women Working as Practical Nurses: Exploring the Connection with Foreign Workers," in Research Committee on the Labor Market, *Changes in Economic Policy and the Labor Market* (Statistical Research Association, August 1991).

Part III

Long-Term Solutions

6

Foreign Workers and Human Rights

1. Long-term Trends and Policy Responses

In the preceding chapters we discussed Japan's medium-term foreign worker policies, such as the work-and-learn program. In the following three chapters, however, I would like to consider the issue from a longer-term perspective.

The long-term situation for foreign workers will be affected by a number of underlying megatrends. The most significant of these are population trends. Most industrialized countries, including Japan, now have rapidly aging populations, and many of them face a long-term population decline as well. Meanwhile, the world population as a whole continues to spiral, due to the pace of population growth in the developing regions of the world such as South Asia, Africa, and Latin America.

So long as there is this contradiction, and the population of the developing countries continues to explode while that of the industrialized nations declines, there are obviously grounds for concern that population will tend to be redistributed from regions with too many people to regions with too few. The process of redistribution will no doubt involve many different types of population shifts including immigration and movements of workers and refugees.

As time goes by, the nature of Japan's foreign worker problem will gradually change. Whereas concern focused initially on the more or less temporary problem of accepting foreign labor, it will eventually come to center on the issue of foreign workers settling down on a permanent basis. While a few nations have admitted foreign workers as bona fide immigrants, all those that have introduced foreign labor on a temporary basis have ultimately been forced to confront problems they had not anticipated, as workers and their families gradually settled down for good. Japan is no exception to this rule, and has already set out down a road from which there can be no turning back.

The problem will be whether Japanese society can adapt to the presence of foreign workers, and vice versa. It is not easy for any society to assimilate and adapt to people of different cultures. There is always confusion, which can manifest itself in racial tension, discord, complications, and discrimination. One prerequisite, if foreign workers are to live in Japanese society with any peace of mind, is that their basic human rights are protected. Yet this will not be enough on its own. Both society and the workers themselves will also have to bear a heavy cost burden, and both sides will have to work to change their attitudes.

It will not be an easy process. If changes are introduced too rapidly, they could provoke a social backlash and obstruct progress toward adaptation. Efforts must first be made to increase the efficiency of industry and restructure the economy to function with a minimum of reliance on low-skilled foreign labor. If Japan then still needs to admit foreign workers, it must fully guarantee their basic human rights.

The best long-term policy the nation can adopt, therefore, is one oriented to a more efficient economic structure and a more enlightened attitude toward the protection of human rights. This means Japan must take a very cautious approach to the acceptance of foreign workers, but also act positively and resolutely to institute more open social systems.

2. International Population Movements and the Foreign Worker Problem

The World Population Explosion

In recent years the world population has been increasing at an accelerating pace. As we have seen, the main reason is the rapid increase in the population of the developing world. Table 6.1 shows predicted world population trends by region. Table 6.1a illustrates population size by region, and b shows the relative distribution of population by region. Figures are United Nations estimates based on 1990 data.

As Table 6.1 shows, the world population stood at 2.52 billion in 1950, increased to 5.29 billion by 1990, and is predicted to reach 8.5 billion in 2025. The growth rate is clearly accelerating.

Table 6.1   Trends and Distribution of World Population by Region

	1950	1990	2000	2025
a. Total World Population (millions)				
Total world	25.2	52.9	62.6	85.0
Industrialized regions	8.3	12.1	12.6	13.5
Developing regions	16.8	40.9	50.0	71.5
Africa	2.2	6.4	8.7	16.0
Latin America	1.7	4.5	5.4	7.6
North America	1.7	2.8	2.9	3.3
East Asia	6.7	13.4	15.1	17.4
South Asia	7.1	17.8	22.0	31.8
Europe	3.9	5.0	5.1	5.2
Oceania	0.1	0.3	0.3	0.4
Soviet Union	1.8	2.9	3.1	3.2
b. Percentage of World Population				
Total world	100.0	100.0	100.0	100.0
Industrialized regions	33.1	22.8	20.2	15.9
Developing regions	66.9	77.2	79.8	84.1
Africa	8.8	12.1	13.8	18.8
Latin America	6.6	8.5	8.6	8.9
North America	6.6	5.2	4.7	3.9
East Asia	26.7	25.2	24.1	20.4
South Asia	28.1	33.6	35.2	37.3
Europe	15.6	9.4	8.1	6.1
Oceania	0.5	0.5	0.5	0.4
Soviet Union	7.2	5.5	4.9	4.1

Source: UN, "World Population Prospects, Estimates and Projections as Assessed in 1990."

During this 75-year period, the population of the industrialized world is expected to increase some 62%, from 830 million to 1.35 billion, whereas the population of the developing world is predicted to increase 325%, from 1.68 billion to 7.15 billion. Consequently, as can be seen from Table 6.1b, the industrialized nations' share of the total world population has fallen from 33.1% to 15.9%, whereas that of the developing nations has risen from 66.9% to 84.1%.

Population is increasing especially rapidly in the South Asian region—particularly India and Pakistan, in Africa, and in Latin America. Meanwhile the relative share of industrialized regions like Europe and North America has fallen dramatically. The proportion of world population accounted for by Europe has plunged from 15.6% to 6.1%, and that of North America has tumbled from 6.6% to 3.9%. Japan is included in the larger region of East Asia, but, as we will see below, the Japanese population is expected to start declining after the turn of the century, and Japan's share of the total world population will also decline sharply.

These enormous changes in the size and structure of the world population are bound to pose major distributional problems for the future.

Rapidly growing populations in the developing countries will exacerbate food shortages, aggravate urban poverty, and contribute to a variety of other problems on both a regional and a global scale. Meanwhile the industrialized nations, whose populations are no longer increasing and in some cases are decreasing, will face labor shortages and have to cope with aging societies.

It is a natural economic phenomenon, under such conditions, that capital and labor should migrate across national borders in search of greater marginal profits. In economic terms, this means capital will flow from the industrialized regions to the developing regions of the world, where marginal profits are higher, and labor will flow from the developing regions to the industrialized regions, where wage levels are higher.

The soaring world population will eventually reach the point where it can no longer be contained by resource redistribution and the world will come up against food resource, energy, and environmental limitations, which will then act to constrain population growth itself. This is bound to lead to a new series of more fundamental problems concerning the redistribution of population and economic opportunities. But we do not have the space to go into this question any more deeply.

Movements of Population Across National Borders

Population movements across borders can take a number of forms. They may involve the migration of workers in search of jobs, or the displacement of refugees for either economic or political reasons.[1] Population movements result largely from redistributions of labor through rational choices corresponding to economic differences and

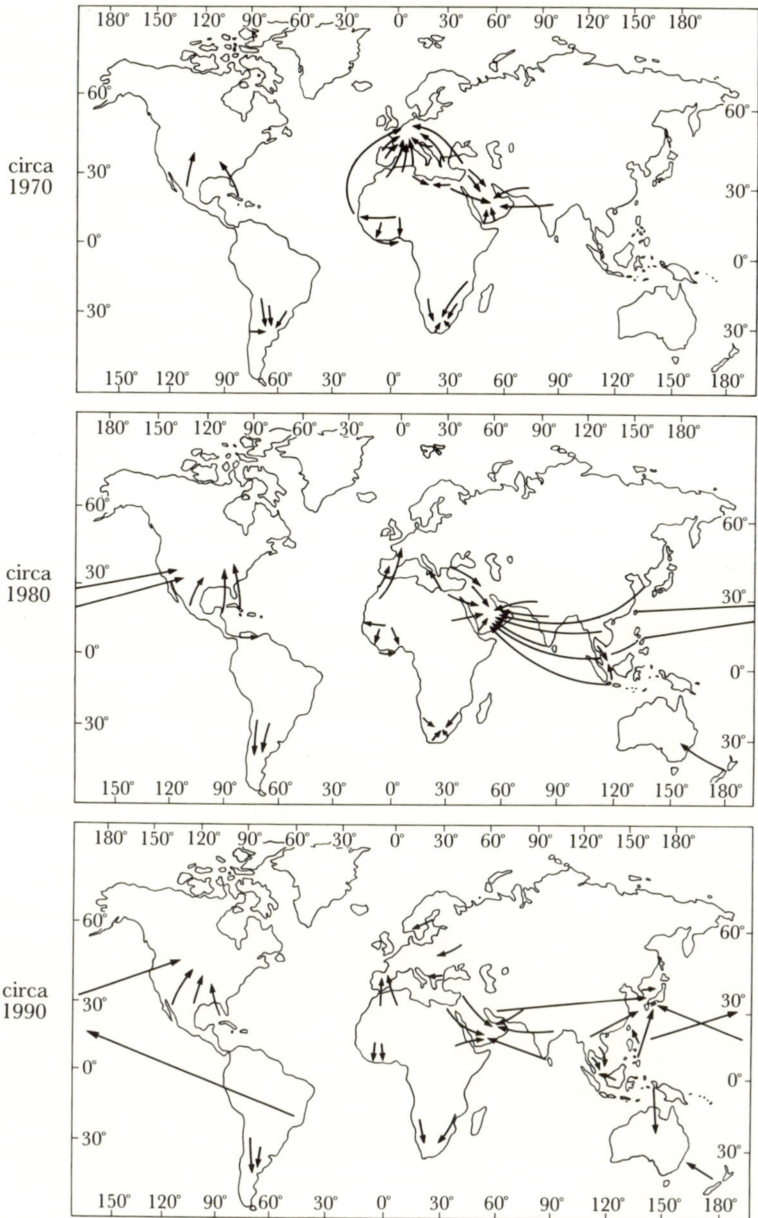

Figure 6.1   Major international migrations of labor

Source: Yasuo Kuwahara, *Workers Migrating Across National Borders* (Iwanami Shoten, 1991); *International Labor Review*, Fall 1989.

opportunities. But individual movements of labor obviously reflect changes in specific, individual conditions, and once a certain flow of labor is established, there seems to be a tendency for the flow to continue to some extent under its own momentum.[2]

Figure 6.1 is an impressionistic illustration of trends in the worldwide flow of labor from the 1970s to the 1990s. The most striking flows of labor from the 1960s to the 1970s were the migration of Turkish, Yugoslavian, and Algerian workers into West European countries like France and Germany, which then faced labor shortages in the wake of sustained periods of rapid growth, and the influx of foreign workers into Saudi Arabia and the other oil-producing countries of the Middle East from neighboring regions.

After the oil crisis of the 1970s, the economies of Germany and the other West European countries took downward turns, and they switched to an exclusionist policy toward foreign labor. By contrast, however, large numbers of foreign workers poured into Saudi Arabia and the other oil-producing nations, not only from neighboring countries but from as far afield as India, the Philippines, Korea, and other parts of Asia, to work on development-related construction projects fueled by the enormous oil revenues of these nations. There was also a large influx of labor from Central America and the Asian countries into the United States during this period.

With the appreciation of the yen after the Plaza Accord in the mid-1980s, the influx of foreign workers into Japan adds a new element to the picture. Meanwhile the flow of labor into the Mid-Eastern oil-producing nations and the United States continues as before, and we also begin to see significant movements of labor from Eastern to Western Europe as a result of the political and economic upheavals in Eastern Europe.

These various movements of labor across national borders are shown in Figure 6.1. More recently, attention has focused on the huge movements of population from the collapsing Soviet Union and neighboring communist nations into Western Europe, refugee migrations in Africa and the Middle East, and population movements in China and other Asian countries.

Increasingly alarmed by the influx of refugees from Eastern Europe and the former Soviet Union, the Western European countries have adopted tougher policies on immigration and foreign labor.[3] Meanwhile the United States has strengthened surveillance of illegal immigration from Mexico and introduced tighter restrictions on immigration from other areas as well.

The population explosion and these trends in the international movement of labor are obviously of great concern to Japan. As an island nation Japan has to some extent been protected from the problems of illegal immigration that have plagued countries which share common borders, but improvements in transportation links mean Japan's geographical isolation no longer serves as an effective barrier.

The greatest pressure for immigration to Japan probably comes from China. The official population of China now exceeds 1.1 billion, and the real figure may be much higher. Over the last few years China has experienced some very uncoordinated economic growth, which has been far more rapid in the coastal regions than in the interior. Hence, despite the fact that movements of population within China are quite rigorously controlled, there has been a precipitate influx of population to the coastal regions due to their burgeoning employment opportunities. And this has given rise to an "overshooting" phenomenon, whereby the influx of population to the regions of higher economic growth has overshot the increase in labor demand. One could say the vast Chinese population, or at least part of it, is now in a slightly unstable state of flux.[4]

The situation in China has inevitably given rise to fears that, if employment opportunities have drawn massive numbers of people from the interior of the country to the coastal regions, at least some of them may start crossing the sea to Japan, where income levels are tens of times higher than those in even the coastal regions of China. While the numbers involved may be very small in terms of the entire Chinese population, such an influx could have an enormous impact on Japan, whose population is only a tenth the size of China's. There are also some grounds for fear that unstable political conditions in China might lead to a wave of refugees from rural areas.

Foreign Workers Are Not Refugees
Such fears have led some to argue forcefully that Japan should close the doors tight and exclude foreign labor altogether. But this argument tends to confuse the problem of Japan's foreign workers with the larger problems of the global population explosion and international movements of labor, and has caused people to draw the wrong conclusions.

While there is certainly a population explosion and increasing international movements of population and labor, neither of these issues has a direct bearing on the influx of foreign labor to nations like Japan. We have already seen how the rapidly increasing influx of foreign workers to Japan in recent years has been due to the mounting demand from Japanese industry. Labor has been drawn into the country by an increase in demand rather than forced on it by pressure from outside. Of course, since labor demand is not perfectly coordinated with the foreign labor supply, there is always going to be some degree of gap between supply and demand.

From the second half of the 1980s up until about 1991, there was basically a large excess of labor demand, but also a certain amount of "overshooting" on the supply side, as symbolized by the crowds of unemployed Iranians congregating in Tokyo's Ueno and Yoyogi Parks. But this oversupply was only a partial and marginal phenomenon, which could not continue for long in the face of contracting demand. Demand had in fact been contracting since 1992, and the balance is now shifting toward an excess of supply. While there will be an increase in the number of foreign workers unemployed due to excessive supply, the level of new immigration by unskilled foreign workers will now probably decline.

Hence there is simply no basis for the argument that Japan must close its doors to foreign labor because it is threatened by the population explosion and increased international movements of labor. The level of foreign labor in Japan has increased only because the demand existed, and we can say that if there had been no demand in the first place, there would have been no influx of foreign workers either.

Refugees, however, are a different matter. They are either fleeing from political or social danger or else being swept along by events. Either way, their movements have nothing to do with domestic labor demand. Refugees enter a nation irrespective of its policy on foreign labor. Conversely, we can say that institutional measures barring the entry of foreign labor would have no effect on refugees. The prevailing wisdom in the world today is that industrialized nations like Japan should do their part in accepting refugees for humanitarian reasons.[5] Particularly since 1982, when it ratified the treaty on the status of refugees, Japan has been increasing the number of refugees it accepts. The expectations of the international community demand that it continue to accept more refugees in the future and fully guarantee their human rights. Japan must be fully resolved to do so.

3. Foreign Workers and Permanent Residence

Foreign Workers Will Inevitably Settle Permanently

So far we have looked at the role of the world population problem and population movements in Japan's foreign worker problem. I have emphasized that the refugee problem and the foreign worker problem are essentially two different issues which should not be confused, and that Japan must come up with appropriate policy responses to each of these problems separately.

But the question of greatest long-term significance is that of foreign workers remaining in Japan and settling down. With such large numbers of foreign workers entering and leaving the country, at least some of them are bound to remain in Japan and build up a presence in society. This has been the experience of all nations that have introduced foreign labor in the past, without exception.[6] Several West European countries, particularly the former West Germany, failed to anticipate, when they introduced foreign labor in response to labor shortages, that these workers would remain and settle down permanently in the country afterwards. Although earnings were higher in the West European countries, the cost of living was also higher, and it was assumed that immigrant workers would not consider it in their best interests to stay in the country for any length of time. They were expected to conform to the pattern of "guest workers," earn high wages for a short period of time, then take their savings back with them to their home countries where the cost of living was lower.[7]

While the majority of foreign workers did return home after relatively short periods of employment, some of them remained, married, and had children, or had their families join them, and their numbers gradually increased. The build-up in numbers occurs through a variety of different channels: relatively formal government programs, as in Germany; informal links, based on family or connections, as in the United States; or brokering agencies such as are common in many of the developing countries that send foreign workers overseas. But once such networks are formed, they tend to go on functioning semi-autonomously so that the influx of foreign workers goes on increasing under its own momentum.[8]

At present, unskilled foreign workers who are in Japan as trainees or under the skills work-training system are in principle not allowed to be accompanied by their families or have their families join them at a later date. Trainees are expected to conform to a model pattern, according to which they come to Japan unaccompanied, return home after acquiring a certain level of skill, and go on to contribute to the development of industry in their home countries.

This model is appropriate so long as it is what the trainees themselves want. But needless to say, no such pattern can be enforced irrespective of the will of the individuals concerned. Whether and whom to marry, having children, and living with one's family are essentially matters of free individual choice, and that freedom of choice must be guaranteed to foreign workers as one of the most basic of human rights.

A number of the illegally employed workers who have entered the Japanese labor market in such large numbers, and the legal foreign workers who have overstayed their visas, are getting married, having children, forming families, and settling down in Japan in increasing numbers. This is the same process that has been experienced in most nations that have introduced foreign labor in the past, and Japan can hardly be the sole exception to the rule. These workers will eventually form a social class of their own, large enough to be impossible to ignore. So Japan has already set out down a path from which it cannot turn back, in the sense that it now has no option but to coexist with these (in effect) new permanent residents.

There is bound to be a certain amount of maladjustment between foreign workers and the societies of their adopted countries. The Turkish workers who have settled down and built up a presence in the former West Germany were unable fully to adapt to German society and eventually formed their own isolated communities in each region of the country. The difficulty of adaptation is symbolized by the language problem. Many of Germany's *Gastarbeiter* are less than fluent in German, which has handicapped their efforts to adapt to society. And the language problem has not been resolved by second-generation foreigners born in Germany, many of whom have failed to master their parents' mother tongues and would be unable to adapt in their parents' countries, making them doubly alienated.

But the problem is not just the inability of foreign workers and their children to adapt to the society. The society itself tends to view them as outsiders, discriminate against them, and effectively alienate them. This mutual maladjustment then compounds the difficulty of the problem. It gives rise to dislike and suspicion, leads to recriminations, defamation, and discrimination, and encourages violence and crime.[9]

The coexistence of heterogeneous groups or classes of people has always and everywhere been one of humanity's most difficult challenges. To resolve these problems fully would mean dismantling all nation-states and ethnic groups and reducing all human interaction to the individual level, which is hardly within the bounds of possibility. Indeed, even on an individual, interpersonal level, it would probably still be just as difficult for people with inherent differences to coexist with one another.

However, while the problem of coexistence can probably never be wholly resolved, that does not mean nothing can be done to stop the situation from getting any worse. The best policy in this regard is to guarantee foreign workers and their families the same basic human rights as citizens, and make sure they do not suffer unfair discrimination or disadvantage in their work or their everyday lives either under the law or in terms of social customs.

Accepting Foreign Workers Must Mean Guaranteeing Their Rights
The most basic human right that foreign workers must be guaranteed is the right to subsistence. Both in their work and in their everyday lives they must have access to conditions that enable them to live in reasonable comfort. This is not generally an issue for foreign workers so long as they remain in good health, but all sorts of difficulties can arise if they are injured, fall ill, or grow too old to work. If their basic needs are to be met even under such adverse conditions, they must be granted various forms of social security, including workers' accident compensation, medical insurance, and pensions. They must not be unfairly discriminated against or exploited, either in their work or in their daily lives—in housing for example. At least these basic rights must be guaranteed. The absence of any one of them makes it difficult for people to live decent lives of the quality all people should be entitled to.

International standards have now been established to guarantee the basic human rights of foreign workers through treaties and recommendations drawn up by international bodies like the United Nations and the International Labor Organization (ILO). The ILO, established in 1919, very early on adopted conventions and recommendations to secure the right to subsistence for immigrant workers, and has continuously worked to establish international standards. The conventions adopted by the ILO to date include the Convention on the

Equal Treatment of Nationals and Foreigners with Regard to Workers' Accident Compensation (Convention 19, 1925), the Convention on the Establishment of an International System for Preserving the Rights of Immigrants Based on Disability, Old Age, Widows and Orphans' Insurance (Convention 48, 1935), the Convention on the Equal Treatment of Nationals and Foreigners with Regard to Social Security (Convention 118, 1962), and the Convention on the Establishment of an International System to Preserve Social Security Rights (Convention 157, 1982). Japan has yet to ratify any of these conventions except number 19.[10]

Convention 48, adopted in 1935, was the first comprehensive convention protecting the rights of immigrant workers. It not only stated the principle of equal treatment for foreigners but also sought to establish an international system for the preservation of rights already obtained and in the process of being obtained. But since the convention was supposed to apply directly, regardless of any prior agreements between the countries concerned, very few nations ratified it and it was largely ineffectual.

Convention 118, which was adopted after World War II, can be said to be a replacement for Convention 48. It demanded reciprocal treatment for all foreigners whose own countries had ratified the convention, except refugees and people with no nationality. It was rather pragmatic in content, in that it did not prescribe income support, and it allowed for a measure of retaliation. Its conditions did not have to be applied to the citizens of any signatory nation which failed to accord equal social security treatment to the citizens of another signatory nation. Consequently many nations ratified the convention, and even today it embodies the basic ILO standards on equal treatment for foreigners.

Compared to the pragmatic and rather unambitious ILO standards, the United Nations treaties are idealistic and positive. The United Nations Universal Declaration of Human Rights, adopted in 1948, declares that all people have the right to receive social security as members of society, without discrimination on the basis of their national or social origins.

The discrepancy between the two sets of standards led the United Nations in 1966 to adopt two legally binding international human rights agreements, Agreement A covering social rights and Agreement B covering the right to liberty. Agreement A was ratified by Japan in 1979 and has so far been ratified by 92 nations in all.

Agreement A pledges all signatory nations to guarantee the rights stipulated by the agreement without distinction as to national or social origin, and prescribes that signatory nations must acknowledge all rights to social insurance and other forms of social security. In other words, the agreement is not reciprocal but sets out a general principle to be applied to all signatory nations across the board. Once ratified, it is supposed to be put into effect immediately.

In 1976, the United Nations adopted a Treaty on the Status of Refugees which states that foreigners and native citizens must be treated equally with regard to income support and social security. Obviously, since the treaty applies to refugees, there can be no reciprocity. Japan ratified this treaty in 1982 and at the same time introduced laws and made institutional changes that have led to real progress in putting the principle into effect.

On December 8, 1990, the United Nations Committee on Human Rights adopted a Treaty to Protect the Rights of Foreign Workers and Their Families. Responding to increased international mobility of labor, the treaty was intended to coordinate the laws and institutional arrangements affecting the acceptance of foreign workers in different countries.[11] It calls for equal treatment of foreigners and native citizens with regard to social security, so long as such treatment is in accord with the laws of the country of residence and with bilateral or multilateral treaties. It prohibits the refusal of emergency medical care to foreigners on the grounds of illegal residence or employment, and stipulates that legal immigrants must be guaranteed equal treatment with regard to housing, insurance, and other services.

Through these ILO and UN treaties, recommendations, and agreements, the international community has made serious efforts to establish international standards for the equal treatment of foreign nationals, and these standards are now beginning to become widely accepted throughout the world.

The principle of equal treatment means foreign workers must be treated equally with regard to basic human rights. Whatever country or region they are working in, and whatever their race or nationality, their status as workers gives them the right to lead decent lives with a modicum of security, and this right should be guaranteed to everyone. All people have the right to be treated equally as citizens of the world.

The ideal of equal treatment is quite clear-cut, and if it could really be implemented there would no longer be any problem, but in the real world things are not that simple. The governments and people of all nations struggle day by day to protect the lives and property of their own people and increase their standard of living. The government ensures the safety of people's lives and property through the instrument of the armed forces and the police, and attempts to expand the economy through various institutional and policy measures. The people in turn support the activities of the government by paying their taxes, and try to raise their standard of living by working. These efforts have enabled nations to set up social security systems whereby all of their citizens can have a certain basic standard of living appropriate to the level of economic growth of the nation.

When foreigners come into a nation, can it immediately offer them the social security its citizens have worked so hard to make available, on exactly the same terms as it offers that support to its own citizens? If that nation has a highly developed social security system while the foreign workers' home countries have little or no system, then treating foreign workers the same as its own citizens unconditionally will amount to a drain of resources. This might be all right if large numbers of its citizens were themselves residing overseas and in turn receiving treatment on equal terms with the citizens of the nations where they live. This is why international agreements advocate reciprocity.

There are differences, however, in the content and scope of social security systems and in nations' levels of economic development; if all nations treated each other on a reciprocal basis, workers crossing national borders would tend to fall foul of the differences between systems. They would miss out on many social security services, and this could jeopardize their right to subsistence, which is their most basic human right. And as we have seen, just leaving foreign workers to their own devices without properly guaranteeing their right to subsistence, under conditions where it is difficult for them to adapt to society, will not only complicate the lives and endanger the human rights of the workers and their families, but also lead to all sorts of social problems and ill effects in the societies of the nations that admit them.

What are Japan's options, then, given the contradiction between, on the one hand, United Nations-type standards that seek to establish universal guarantees of basic human rights and, on the other hand, mutual reciprocity agreements between individual nations each subject to its own resource limitations? We must respect the unique conditions that prevail in our own country and, with due regard to resource limitations, make the greatest possible effort to guarantee the basic human rights of all people, whether native citizens or foreigners. Unless we make such an effort, there is a grave danger that many foreign workers will be caught between different systems and left stranded without any guarantees of even the most basic standards of life.

4. The Basic Human Rights of Foreign Workers

Seven Rights Foreign Workers Must Be Guaranteed

I have argued for some time past that there are seven basic rights which are prerequisite to foreign workers being able to live and work in reasonable comfort. These are: workers' accident compensation, unemployment compensation, medical security, the right to education, the right not to be discriminated against in housing, the right to a pension, and the right to vote in local elections. It may be thought idealistic to try and grant foreign workers all these rights, or that they do not even deserve them. Yet anyone can imagine how, if one were to work overseas for a long period of time, the absence of any of the above rights would make one's own life and work extremely uncomfortable. Japanese citizens have all these rights guaranteed to them as a matter of course, so they tend to take their importance somewhat for granted.

How Far Does Japan's Constitution Guarantee Foreign Workers' Rights?

Since the Japanese Constitution contains no clearly worded definition of the status of foreign workers, the question of whether they are entitled to enjoy the basic human rights guaranteed by the constitution becomes entirely a matter of interpretation.[12]

Chapter III of the constitution defines basic human rights such as the right to equality (Article 14) and the right to subsistence (Article 25), but the chapter is headed "Rights and Duties of the People," and interpretations differ as to whether these rights and duties are limited to Japanese nationals or whether they also apply to foreigners.

One interpretation is that "people" means citizens of Japan, and none of these rights applies to foreigners. But there is also a "partial application theory" which holds that provisions beginning with the phrase "all people" apply only to Japanese citizens whereas those that begin "whosoever" can be extended to foreigners. There is also an "application based on content theory" which holds that some rights can be extended to foreigners, depending on their substance. Judicial precedents from very soon after the establishment of the constitution took the view that human rights guarantees did apply to foreigners, and in recent years there has been wide support for the interpretation that basic human rights guarantees as prescribed by Chapter III of the constitution apply equally to foreign residents of Japan, other than those rights whose nature dictates that they apply only to Japanese citizens.[13]

Following this interpretation, then, some of the various basic human rights defined by the constitution are guaranteed only to Japanese, while others apply equally to foreigners. Specifically, it is generally considered that, owing to their nature, voting rights (Article 15), the right to subsistence (Article 25), the right to education (Article 26), and the right to work (Article 27) apply only to Japanese citizens, whereas the other rights must basically be guaranteed to foreigners as well—namely Articles 13 (respect for the individual), 14 (the principle of equality), 16 (the right to petition), 18 (prohibition of bondage and involuntary servitude), 19 (freedom of thought and conscience), 20 (freedom of religious belief), 21 (freedom of assembly, marriage, and expression, and the protection of the privacy of communication), 22 (freedom to reside where one chooses and change one's occupation), 23 (academic freedom), 24 (dignity of the individual in family relations and equality of the sexes), 28 (workers' rights to organize and bargain collectively), 29 (the right to own or hold property), and 31 to 40 (restrictions on the state's right to imprison, try, and punish people).[14]

There is little room for disagreement about the fact that the rights related to individual freedom and equality and the judicial procedure guarantees are basic rights that must be guaranteed to all people irrespective of whether or not they are Japanese citizens. But creating the conditions for foreign workers in Japan to be able to live decent lives of the same quality as Japanese nationals will entail guaranteeing them at least some of the other rights which are often considered to apply to Japanese only.

The constitution declares that "all citizens have the right to lead lives of a basic minimum standard of health and culture. The state must work for the advancement and improvement of social welfare, social security and public health in all areas of life." If foreign workers are to be able to lead such lives, they must be guaranteed the rights defined by Articles 25 (the right to subsistence and the duty of the state to work for social progress and improve the standard of living), 26 (the right to receive an education and the duty of the state to provide it), and 15 (the right to vote)—or at least the right to vote in local elections.

I stated above that for foreign workers in Japan to lead lives of the same quality as Japanese citizens requires that they be guaranteed at least seven basic rights. Guaranteeing all of these rights in full will of course involve all sorts of practical difficulties. As we saw in the interpretation of the constitution, there will be theoretical problems in determining whether there is any legal basis for guaranteeing rights to foreign workers even if they have to be guaranteed to Japanese citizens. And even where it is thought desirable to extend certain rights to foreign workers, there will be cases where Japan cannot very well do so unilaterally in the absence of reciprocal guarantees from other countries. Japan does not have limitless resources to expend on the provision of social security. All countries have a duty to provide security to their own citizens and must allocate their resources on a preferential basis. Public opinion will not allow them to pour resources into improving welfare facilities for foreigners at the expense of the nation's economic welfare and prosperity.

Bearing in mind these problems and difficulties, I would now like to consider these seven symbolic rights, looking at the actual situation and pointing out some specific problems that may arise.

Workers' Accident Compensation

Workers' accident compensation is one of the most basic rights that foreign workers must be guaranteed if they are to work in Japan with any peace of mind. Provisions must be made so that, if they are injured or fall ill by reason of their work, they can receive the medical care and treatment they need until such time as they are able to start work again. The right to workers' accident compensation is one of the most immediate and important rights.

Japan, in common with most other industrialized countries, guarantees all workers the right to accident compensation through the Workers' Compensation Insurance Act. Workers' compensation insurance entitles beneficiaries to receive a basic salary irrespective of the length of time they have been paying into the system. Naturally, the insurance premiums are paid by the employer. The law makes no distinction between Japanese and foreigners in the right to receive benefits. Benefits include: medical care compensation (medical treatment costs), compensation for business suspension (wages for the number of days off work), sickness and injury compensation pension (where treatment extends for a long period), disability compensation (where injuries persist after treatment), survivors' compensation (in case of death), and funeral costs.

Officially, then, the workers' compensation insurance system guarantees compensation to Japanese and foreigners alike, and even illegal workers are entitled to the same benefits.[15] However, it has long since been pointed out that there are a number of problems in actually implementing the system. I would like to refer to two of these problems.

One problem is the special transnational paperwork required for foreign workers to receive benefits overseas. In principle, workers' compensation benefits can be paid across national borders, and in many cases they actually are. Most foreign workers injured at work tend to return home after receiving some initial medical treatment in Japan, where the level of medical care is relatively high. But there appear to be many unresolved problems in this system. The paperwork for applications, billing, and payments outside the country is very complicated, and misunderstandings arise with health care systems in workers' home countries.[16]

Another problem applies particularly to illegal workers. Their status means they face deportation from Japan if their existence comes to light. Hence illegal workers who suffer injuries at work tend to conceal their injuries for fear of exposure. With the implementation of the Revised Immigration Law in June 1990 this tendency has grown stronger because the new law takes a much harsher line toward illegal workers and makes it a crime to encourage illegal employment. While workers may be entitled to accident compensation on paper, they still tend to conceal industrial injuries for fear of deportation, and suffer tragic harm as a result.[17]

This can be seen as symbolizing the contradiction in the current system. Japan must systematically improve its foreign worker policy through a work-and-learn program, as I outlined above, and thereby reduce the level of illegal employment. But at the same time Japanese society, including the administration and private industry, must firmly commit itself to providing full medical care and compensation to foreign workers who suffer injuries at work, even if they are illegally employed, so as to avoid potential tragedy.

Unemployment Compensation and Income Support
The next problem facing foreign workers is whether they are eligible for social security benefits if they should lose their jobs or otherwise find themselves destitute.

Japanese nationals whose employers have taken out employment insurance under the Employment Insurance Act can receive unemployment benefits in the event that they lose their jobs. Foreign workers properly qualified to work in Japan can also receive benefits in principle, though in actual fact benefits are granted only to permanent residents, long-term Korean residents in Japan, and dependents of Japanese citizens.[18] All other foreign workers are officially obliged to return home if they become unemployed.[19] Unemployment benefits are not available to illegal foreign workers either.

As to income support, Japanese nationals can apply for and receive a basic living allowance under the Livelihood Protection Act if they have no other means of support. Foreigners used to be eligible under the old Livelihood Protection Act of 1946, but they are excluded from the act presently in force. The Livelihood Protection Act embodies the right to subsistence as defined by Article 25 of the constitution, but, as we saw above, the current authoritative interpretation of the right to subsistence holds that it applies only to Japanese nationals, so foreigners are effectively barred from receiving livelihood protection.

On the other hand foreigners, and even illegal foreign workers, are generally entitled to a number of welfare benefits—child benefits, disability benefits, mental infirmity benefits, and old age pensions. Furthermore, with Japan's ratification of the 1979 International Agreement on Human Rights and its signing of the 1982 Treaty on the Status of Refugees, foreigners are now able to receive child benefits.[20]

The application of Japan's social security policy to foreigners is still uncoordinated. This seems to stem basically from the contradiction between the view that the right to subsistence as defined by the constitution does not apply to foreigners and more fundamental international human rights standards. But it is essential that foreign workers are accorded the right to subsistence if they are to be guaranteed a basic minimum standard of life.

Medical Security

The right to medical security is an important part of the basic human right to subsistence. All Japanese citizens are covered by the medical insurance system. People qualify for insurance under one of two systems: either they can contribute to a health insurance policy taken out by their employer under the Health Insurance Act, or they can enroll directly in the national health insurance system under the National Health Insurance Act.

Most foreign workers who are legally entitled to work also contribute to health insurance taken out by their employers and receive the same benefits as Japanese citizens.[21] Illegal foreign workers are obviously not covered by medical insurance because enrolling in either system would immediately reveal their whereabouts and result in deportation.

Businesses with five or more employees, and even small businesses with fewer employees if they are incorporated, are obliged by law to take out medical insurance for all full-time employees, with premiums shared equally between employer and employee. In actual fact, however, non-incorporated businesses often do not fulfill their legal obligations to provide insurance, with the result that large numbers of workers are not in fact covered by their employers' medical insurance systems. It can be conjectured that many foreign workers fall into this category as well.[22]

The only way these people can cover themselves is by enrolling in the national health insurance system as individuals, but enrollment is conditional on continuous residence in a city, town, or village for a period of more than a year. Foreigners must have a certificate of alien registration, which automatically excludes illegal workers. And many foreigners appear not to enroll in the national health insurance system because they feel the cost is excessively high.

The picture that emerges from this survey of the health insurance system, then, is that neither foreign workers working in small companies, who have been in Japan less than a year, and their families, or illegal foreign workers, can receive medical insurance benefits. Yet their living conditions make them the very people most in danger of falling ill, and they stand in most need of protection. The fact that they are excluded from medical security constitutes a major problem for Japan's medical insurance system.

The Right to Receive Education

The right to receive an education is also an important basic human right. Along with the right to work, it can be said to be a prerequisite for people to "maintain the minimum standards of wholesome and cultured living" (Article 25). If the people are to make full use of their abilities, enjoy the fruits of the nation's economic development, and lead healthy and cultured lives in society, it is essential that they receive an appropriate education that enables them to make full use of their latent potential. However, the right to receive an education as defined by the constitution is generally construed to apply only to Japanese citizens, not to foreigners.

Foreign workers face two problems with regard to education. They need education for themselves and education for their children.

The most necessary form of education for the foreign workers themselves is Japanese language education. This falls into the category of adult education or social education, and is therefore rather different from the compulsory education generally conceived to be a basic human right. However, Japanese language ability is the most basic essential skill foreigners need to survive in Japanese society, so it ranks with compulsory school education in terms of its importance. We looked at my own proposal for Japanese language education for foreign workers in Chapter 6, so there is no need to go into the question any further here.

While the right to receive education and the obligation of the state to provide it, as defined by the constitution, do not officially apply to the children of foreign workers, nevertheless it is the local schools that face the reality of the problem, and in many localities the schools are providing a variety of educational services to the children of foreign workers.[23]

But education is expected to become an extremely important policy issue as more and more foreign workers come to settle down in the country. Public education services and guidance to the education system must be made fully available to the children of legally employed foreigners and great care taken to ensure that they are not disadvantaged in comparison with Japanese children. Policy consideration must also be given to assuring that foreign children are not at a disadvantage when they apply for jobs after graduating from school. At the same time Japan must come to grips with the problem of providing a basic essential education to the children of illegal workers and those who have overstayed their visas, so that these children can grow up to become functional members of society. We have reached the stage where both ethical and basic human rights considerations demand serious institutional changes.

The Right Not to Be Discriminated Against in Housing

The housing problem is one of the most serious problems confronting foreign workers in their everyday lives. It is also a grave problem for many Japanese citizens. The problem basically centers on the availability of housing in terms of quantity, quality, and price. The government does direct some public resources towards improving the availability of housing. Government policy includes the provision of public housing, public promotion of housing construction projects, and public housing loans. But few foreign workers can enjoy the benefits of this policy. Public housing is available to foreigners, but basically only to permanent residents and to some others in special cases.

For many foreign workers, an even more serious housing problem is the discrimination they face in renting private apartments.[24] Some local authorities are trying to eliminate such discrimination by issuing rules and using moral suasion to raise people's awareness of the problem.[25] Discrimination in housing threatens the livelihoods of foreign workers, who already suffer from enough uneasiness in their lives without it. But eliminating discrimination will require legislative relief measures rather than just attempts to heighten the awareness of society.

Pension Rights

Pensions are one of the most basic social security rights, affording workers a sense of security throughout their working lives.

Japan has a national pension insurance system that covers all its citizens, and all adults over the age of 20 resident in Japan are basically obliged to pay contributions. There is no distinction as to nationality, and in principle even illegal foreign workers are eligible to enroll in the system on the basis that they are resident in Japan.

Employees in businesses covered by the welfare pension system share pension contributions equally with their employers. The system insures both employees and their dependents. People working in non-incorporated businesses with fewer than five employees, however, since these businesses are not covered by the welfare pension system, have to enroll in the national pension system and pay the contributions on their own.

Whichever system citizens pay into, they are entitled to receive an old-age pension from the age of 60, which guarantees them stability in their retirement. The same conditions apply to foreign workers as to Japanese, and all foreigners resident in Japan are obliged either to enroll in the national pension system individually or to pay welfare pension insurance contributions if their employer is eligible for the system.

However, many foreigners face difficulties in actually receiving pensions or are treated unfairly. In order to receive an old-age pension you have to have paid into the system for a minimum of 25 years. You cannot receive a pension unless you have lived in Japan for at least 25 years and paid pension insurance premiums continuously over that period.

Most foreigners work in Japan only for a relatively short period of time, and very few for as long as 25 years. Yet most foreign workers, however short their period of stay in the country, are forced to pay into either the welfare pension insurance or national pension insurance system for the duration. Foreigners who reach retirement age in Japan are still not eligible for a pension if they have not been enrolled in the system for long enough. And the pension contributions they have paid in Japan cannot be refunded. An even more serious problem for such people is that when they return to their home countries after many years in Japan, they find they are also disqualified from receiving a pension at home because they have not paid into their own countries' pension system for long enough either. Even if they are lucky enough to qualify for a pension at home, the fact that they have not paid contributions for long enough often means they can only receive a much smaller pension, and they end up severely disadvantaged.

This problem could basically be resolved if Japan and the countries concerned were to draw up international agreements for mutual fulfilment of pension claims. Quite a number of nations have already signed such international agreements on pensions with other countries in order to protect foreign workers and people posted overseas by their employers from losing their pension rights.[26] But the Japanese government has yet to conclude any such agreements, and there is at this stage no means of redressing the loss. The pension problem acts as a major disincentive to foreign workers with specialist skills and knowledge to remain in Japan for any length of time, though it would be to Japan's advantage if they did. The lack of proper international pension agreements could therefore be a major disadvantage not only to the foreign workers concerned but also to the nation.

In addition, there is a considerable danger that large numbers of foreign workers will fall through the net and fail to enroll in the national pension system. Most foreign workers without specialist skills or knowledge are employed in very small businesses, many of which are not covered by the welfare pension insurance system. While they are supposed to enroll in the national pension system as individuals, it is thought that many opt out of it to avoid the burden of paying the contributions.[27]

In addition, workers employed on short-term contracts, and those subject to overseas pension laws, are not covered by the system even when their employers are. In the latter case the criteria for exclusion are by no means clear, and there is a danger that employers may take advantage of these workers to save on pension contributions and cut costs.[28]

Voting Rights

For the citizens of any nation with a democratic electoral system, voting rights are an essential basic human right. In Japan, as we have seen, the right to vote in local and national elections, including the right to stand for election, are considered to be the sole prerogative of Japanese citizens, and not applicable to resident foreigners.

But this view is by no means unassailable. There may well be grounds for enfranchising permanently resident foreigners, and for allowing foreigners at least to vote in local elections, if not general elections.

Foreigners permanently resident in Japan, while they may still have overseas nationality, do not differ from Japanese citizens in any other respect. They work in Japan for their entire lives, contribute to the Japanese economy and society, pay their taxes and, as citizens of the nation, are subject to the same restraints and obligations as Japanese. As taxpayers, and as citizens with duties and limitations, it is natural that they should have some say, through the ballot box, in the local politics that directly influences their civic lives, and giving these people the vote is hardly likely to cause any particular inconvenience. I myself feel it is perfectly natural that foreign workers who are permanent residents should be allowed to vote in local elections.[29]

This has been a question of interest and contention in many countries that have welcomed foreign workers in the past. Both Sweden and the Netherlands allow foreign workers the vote subject to certain restrictions, while the issue is now being debated in Germany.[30] In Japan too, some local authorities are showing mounting interest in the question.[31]

Welcoming Foreign Workers as Equals: Institutional and Social Responses

Once foreign workers have been accepted into the country, if they are to live in Japanese society as equals they will have to be guaranteed the same basic human rights as Japanese workers. We have looked at seven examples of such basic rights. But these rights on their own will not give them the institutional guarantees they need to live decent lives. There are a number of other essential rights as well. The freedom to choose one's occupation and the right not to be discriminated against in employment, for example, are important rights that we have not touched on here.

The seven rights discussed above are mainly concerned with social security, and together constitute the right to subsistence. Foreign workers are basically eligible for workers' accident compensation, unemployment security, medical security, and pension rights, but are not guaranteed the right to education, the right not to be discriminated against in housing, or voting rights. And illegal workers, while they may theoretically be eligible for workers' accident compensation and medical insurance, cannot in most cases obtain it due to the principle of exclusion. Foreigners are legally obliged to pay pension contributions, but in most cases they do not pay into the system for long enough, and so do not qualify for pensions. So there are many areas where even institutional guarantees of the rights of foreign workers are inadequate, and they lack the institutional protection they need to be able to live comfortably in Japanese society.

To guarantee that foreign workers are accepted into society as equals, then, the most fundamental task is to institute legislative and policy reforms. This is the very first issue Japan will have to resolve, and the prime obligation it will have to meet, if it wants to be seen as an "open nation" in the international community. Applying the spirit of "equality under the law" as defined by the Japanese constitution to the daily lives and specific job circumstances of the foreigners living and working in Japan, and realizing this equality, will mean overhauling all the various laws that pertain to their lives and jobs and carrying out the necessary legislative reforms that will enable their basic rights to be honored.

Yet institutional changes alone will not be enough to assure that foreign workers can live comfortably in Japanese society, free from anxiety, on an equal level with Japanese citizens. Of equal or even greater importance will be the customs and values of Japanese society. Foreign workers' accommodation to society will depend on the attitudes of the Japanese people and to what extent they can really welcome foreigners as equals.

People's ability to accept foreigners is dictated by their way of life and way of looking at the world, their way of thinking, and their instinctive reactions to things. It cannot very well be instituted through legislation, nor is it amenable to sheer logical analysis. Attitudes do not change easily. They are deeply rooted in the national culture, which is cultivated over the centuries of a nation's history.

I do not mean to get into a discussion of comparative culture, but merely wish to consider how people understand the idea of equality with foreigners or indeed the concept of equality itself.

Usually people feel a sense of security and familiarity with those essentially similar to themselves or sharing a similar burden. Hence they are liable to feel wary and suspicious of people who are different or have nothing in common with them. These human emotions are perfectly natural and have been basically true of all people throughout history and regardless of nationality or race.

Foreigners are seen by the natives of any country to be different, and to have relatively little in common with them. This may not present a problem if the number of foreigners is small, but if numbers start increasing at a faster rate, it is bound to increase people's fears and apprehensions. This will be all the more so if the new immigrants are seen to have a direct effect on people's lives and work. Unease and wariness can easily turn into resistance and violence, and when the object of such fears is in a weaker position, it can also lead to discrimination and oppression.

There are two ways of reducing the ill effects of social maladjustment to a minimum. One is for the nation to increase the level of immigration very slowly and gradually. It takes time for people to adjust culturally and socially, and if the numbers increase gradually it gives them time to adapt at their own pace. This is why I have advised Japan to exercise caution in accepting foreign workers. Another way to facilitate integration is to do everything possible to increase contact and exchange between Japanese and foreigners in everyday life, at work and elsewhere, so as to further mutual understanding. Contacts can be furthered, to some extent in a planned way, on a variety of levels, in local communities, in companies, in schools, and in families. The more effective this mutual contact, exchange, and understanding, the less social friction there will be and the more foreign workers the nation will be able to accept.

The essence of integration is mutual adaptation, adjustment, and understanding, so that people become increasingly able to recognize each other as equal individuals. This dissolution of cultural friction is a phenomenon we can see happening all the time, not just between people of different races but between people from the same nation but different regional or professional backgrounds. Indeed married couples commonly experience the same process. People's allergy to different cultures gradually decreases as they build up shared experience, come to know more about each other and come to have more in common. As part of this process they also come to recognize each other as equals.

The ultimate litmus test of whether someone had been able to overcome the cultural gulf separating Japanese and foreigners, and had really reached the point of recognizing foreigners as equals, would be whether he or she could accept the idea of marrying someone of another race.

To avoid misunderstanding, I should point out that marriage is an agreement between individuals, and the decision to marry is entirely subject to the free will of the individuals concerned. In other words, however much one may like or dislike someone's prospective partner, it is entirely a matter of individual choice and such a choice cannot be criticised as being discriminatory, as this would intrude on the free will of the individual. However, when it comes to marriage between members of specific groups or social classes such as Japanese and foreigners, it is a different story. If a marriage were not approved of for some generalized reason such as the partner's nationality, while the people concerned would of course be free to make that decision, we would have to conclude that the group to which they belonged had failed to inculcate an adequate regard for the people from the other group as equal individuals.

It is hard to say how long it takes to create an environment where people readily approve of intermarriage between different social groups, but it seems to take a long time, even if the two groups live in the same country or region and there is a considerable amount of exchange and experience of living and working together. Even in places where there have been tens or hundreds of years of such experience, the problems that go with assimilation have sometimes been very slow to melt away.

Understanding mutual differences, accepting people as equals while respecting their differences, and building a relationship of equals is as difficult as it is important a task. Once such an atmosphere of acceptance pervades society, the foreign worker problem will disappear in the course of ordinary economic and social activity. But so long as people lack such attitudes, the process of integration will throw up endless problems, which will demand careful attention and enormous energy to resolve.

The Cost of Accepting Foreign Workers
The conditions discussed above are fundamental to the creation of a society in which foreigners can live in reasonable comfort and peace of mind. It is easy to talk about these conditions, but it will not necessarily be easy to bring them about. This will entail enormous material costs and a considerable effort of will.

Providing foreign workers with the conditions that will enable them to enjoy the same level of social security as Japanese citizens will normally incur much higher unit costs. Even if Japan provides social security benefits through reciprocal arrangements with the sender countries, the cost to a country like Japan, with its higher standard of living and greater social costs, is bound to be higher. If, on the other hand, Japan were to provide foreigners with income support, medical insurance, and so on without such reciprocal agreements, just out of a sense of obligation to protect their human rights, it would entail an even greater drain on resources. Providing housing and social infrastructure will involve enormous costs as well.[32]

These are some of the material costs. But as we saw in the example of marriage, there will also be mental costs, in the sense that people will have to modify their values and lifestyle. These intangible costs can often be greater than the tangible, material costs, and may well provoke a similar degree of social backlash.

It goes without saying that accepting foreign workers will bring benefits as well as costs. As we discussed in some detail in Chapter 2, foreign labor confers many economic advantages on Japan. It helps ease the bottleneck in the labor supply, increases economic activity, and reduces inflationary pressure on the economy. There is also the intangible benefit of a richer cultural diversity.

The economic benefits will be felt most directly by the firms and industries accepting foreign labor, but the bulk of the costs will have to be borne by society as a whole. It can be argued that this imbalance should be rectified by making the firms and industries that benefit most directly bear the lion's share of the social costs. One idea that has been put forward is to levy a tax on industry for the employment of unskilled foreign workers. This would in fact kill two birds with one stone, by acting to control the indiscriminate introduction of foreign workers as a cheap source of labor.

However, it will not be easy to calculate the social costs, and there would be practical difficulties in imposing the whole cost burden on industry. Social costs tend by their nature to increase dynamically. Some foreign workers will eventually settle down and numbers will gradually increase. Their rate of entry to the country tends to depend on an informal network of friends and relatives, and so long as this network continues to operate, numbers will tend to increase of their own accord. Hence we can anticipate an acceleration in both the number of foreigners entering the country and the number settling down, which will give rise to all sorts of problems. The resultant social costs will increase dynamically, so they cannot all be passed on to employers at the outset.

Social costs are bound to increase at an accelerating rate through this dynamic process, and the burden to society will ultimately be enormous. These costs cannot and must not be avoided. They are essential to the formation of a just and open society in which foreign workers are able to live decent and comfortable lives free from anxiety.

If such an open society can indeed be formed and sustained, our only concern will be how to minimize the costs incurred in the process. And the best way to do this will be to raise the productivity of Japanese industry and create an economic structure that does not need to depend on low-skilled or unskilled foreign labor. This will be discussed in detail in the following chapter.

Notes

[1] Council on Population Problems, Ministry of Health and Welfare Population Problems Research Institute, "International Movements of Population" (1993), gives a graphic summary of migrations of population into and out of Japan and other major world nations. Tomomi Otsuka, "The Politics and Economics of International Labor Movements" (Taxation and Accountancy Association, 1993), provides a comprehensive overview of the experience of different nations and the theory of international labor movements. Katsu Yanaihara and Tatsushi Yamagata, eds., *International Migrations of Labor in Asia* (Asian Economy Research Institute Monograph Series, 1992), gives a detailed description of international migrations of labor in the Asian countries and of labor-related policies.

[2] Kirio Morita, *International Movements of Labor* (University of Tokyo Press, 1987), part II. Kazuaki Okabe, *The Arrival of the Multiracial Society* (Ochanomizu Shobo, 1991), chapter 1. Useful data on this problem can be found in papers submitted to the OECD International Conference on Migration, Rome, March 13–15, 1991, and to the UN Expert Group Meeting on Cross-National Labor Migration in Asia: Implications for Local and Regional Development, Nagoya, November 5–8, 1990. Yasuo Kuwahara has done several systematic studies of the subject: *Workers Migrating Across Borders* (Iwanami, 1991); "Formation and Development of the Labor Migration System" and "Dynamics of Population Migration in the Asia-Pacific Region," in Japan Labor Research Organization, *Frontiers of International Labor Migration* (March 1993), chapters 1 and 2.

[3] Philip L. Martin, "EC-92 and Immigration Issues in Europe," October 1990, mimeo.

[4] China's rapid economic growth over the last few years has given rise to serious problems: as productivity, supporting economic growth, has increased in the rural agricultural sector that contains the bulk of the population, it has generated a huge labor surplus which has increased the pressure for population to flow out of these regions. The Chinese government has tried to promote labor exports, i.e., sending workers overseas, to help lessen the effects of this structural anomaly, but the policy is unlikely to bring about a fundamental resolution of the problem. A longer-term strategy for solving the labor surplus would be to take institutional steps to raise the quality of the

workforce and to promote economic growth itself. Zhang Ji-Xung, "China's Labor Allocation Strategy and Labor Migration, and Its Links to Regional Development Strategy," in Labor Market Research Committee, *Frontiers of International Labor Migration* (Japan Labor Research Organization, 1993).

[5] The major problem with accepting refugees in Japan is that Japanese society has never fostered the kind of open-minded attitudes that would encourage people to accept them as permanent residents. Hiroshi Honma, *The Nature of the Refugee Problem* (Iwanami Shoten, 1990).

[6] Hiroaki Suzuki, "Problems Arising from the Influx of Foreign Workers: the Limitations of West European Precedents," in Conference on Social Policy, ed., Annual Report no. 34, *Japanese Firms and Foreign Workers* (Ochanomizu Shobo, 1990).

[7] Shinobu Sato, "Structure of the Gastarbeiter Age," *Ohara Journal of Research into Social Problems*, no. 413, April 1993.

[8] Japan Labor Research Organization, "Policy Issues Concerning the Foreign Labor Problem: A Critical Examination of Current Policy in the Major Labor-Accepting Countries" (March 1991), provides a useful introduction to the situation in France, West Germany, the U.S.A., Australia, and Singapore, and looks at their experiences and the issues they face.

[9] National Police Agency, ed., *Police White Paper 1990*, points out that Japan's increasing crime rate parallels the increase in the level of immigration of foreign workers to Japan. But the increase in crime should be seen as reflecting social maladjustment due to the absence of a social infrastructure appropriate to the acceptance of foreign workers.

[10] Japan has as yet ratified only Convention No. 19.

[11] "International Convention on the Protection of the Rights of All Migrant Workers and Members of Their Families," December 18, 1990.

[12] Ministry of Foreign Affairs, Treaties Bureau, Legal Section, Legislation Research Group, *The Legal Position of Foreigners in Japan* (Nihon Kajo Shuppan, 1993), Commentary.

[13] Ibid., pp. 1–2.

[14] Ibid., p. 2.

[15] Kazuaki Tezuka, "Employment of Foreign Workers: The Situation in the Tokyo Metropolitan Region and Osaka," *Chiba Daigaku Hogaku Ronshu*, vol. 5, no. 2 (February 1991), reports that in Tokyo and Osaka the majority of foreign workers are eligible for workers' accident compensation insurance.

[16] Tsutomu Ouchi et al., "A Study of Systems for Accepting Foreign Workers into Society" (NIRA Study Series), National Institute for Research and Advancement 1990, page 12. Akira Takafuji, "Foreign Workers and Japan's Social Security Law," in Social Security Research Institute, ed., *Foreign Workers and Social Security* (University of Tokyo Press, 1991), chapter 1.

[17] See chapter 2.

[18] Takafuji, op. cit., pp. 10–11.

[19] Ministry of Labor, Employment Security Bureau, ed., "A Manual of Foreign Labor Problems," Labor Administration Research Institute, 1991.

[20] Takafuji, op. cit., pp. 10–11.

[21] Ouchi et al., op. cit., p. 62.

[22] Takafuji, op. cit., pp. 12–13.

[23] National Institute for Research and Advancement (NIRA), "Study of Acceptance and Coexistence with Foreign Workers" (NIRA Study Series), 1990, chapter 3. "Attempting to Scale Language Barriers—Increasing Presence of Foreign Children in the Classroom," *Asahi Shimbun*, June 15, 1991.

[24] Housing and the search for rented accommodation is one of the most difficult problems facing foreign workers. Tokyo Metropolitan Labor Research Institute, "Employment of Foreign Workers in the City of Tokyo," 1991.

[25] NIRA, op. cit., pp. 66–86.

[26] Ouchi et al., op. cit., pp. 10–12.

[27] Takafuji, op. cit., pp. 13–14.

[28] Ouchi et al., op. cit., p. 11.

[29] New Zealand accords foreigners the right to vote in national elections.

[30] Social Security Research Institute, ed., *Foreign Workers and Social Security* (University of Tokyo Press, 1991), chapters 6 and 10. "Foreigners and Voting Rights," *Asahi Shimbun*, January 7, 1992.

[31] NIRA, op. cit., page 67.

[32] Special Subcommittee, Committee to Study the Influence of Foreign Workers on the Labor Situation (chair, Koichiro Yamaguchi), "Social Costs Accompanying the Acceptance of Foreign Workers" (Interim Report, June 26, 1992), points out that while the social costs currently borne by the Japanese government and local authorities are lower than in Europe, they will grow larger as unemployment increases due to economic recession, and foreign workers increasingly become permanent residents. Meanwhile, the Research Group on the Consequences of Accepting Foreign Workers (chair, Hiroyuki Chuma) attempts an estimate of the long-term economic costs and benefits of accepting foreign workers. Including general administrative services, education, and housing costs as social costs, the group concludes that, if the influx continued, in a worst-case scenario the annual costs could amount to 6.3 trillion yen (Y58,000 per annum for each Japanese citizen) by the year 2050, since costs would increase cumulatively over the long term due to the continuing increase in the numbers of foreign workers and their families. On the other hand, if foreign workers were to enter the country on a rotational basis or as temporary workers and did not settle down, the social cost burden could be reduced to a minimum. Sanwa Research Institute, "Analysis of the Economic Costs and Benefits Accompanying the Acceptance of Foreign Workers," April 1992.

7

Structural Reform

1. The Labor Shortage and Structural Reform

Another important issue behind the debate on Japan's acceptance of foreign workers is the trend toward a decline in the nation's population and fears that this will result in a shrinking workforce and a labor shortage. People fear that Japan will be forced to introduce foreign labor to compensate. I would now like to consider these concerns over the future labor force, and the question of how to respond to the problem, in some detail.

The Japanese Population Is Declining over the Long Term

Japan's birthrate plunged rapidly in the immediate postwar years, but recently it has shown signs of declining even further. The trend can be verified from statistics for the fertility rate, which is a measure of the average number of children born to an individual woman over her lifetime. Figure 7.1 shows the total fertility rate of the Japanese population from just after World War II to the present day.

Immediately after the war, Japan's total fertility rate was over 4. In other words, women at that time were bearing, on average, more than four children over their lifetimes. But over the following 10 years the fertility rate declined sharply to reach a level of 2.0. For some time, the rate continued to fluctuate around this level, which would have maintained the Japanese population at a constant size. From the late 1970s, however, it started to decline noticeably, falling even more sharply after 1985, and by 1992 it had dropped to 1.50.

A number of studies have sought to establish why the birthrate should have declined so markedly in recent years, but the reason remains elusive. According to a forecast based on 1991 estimates of fu-

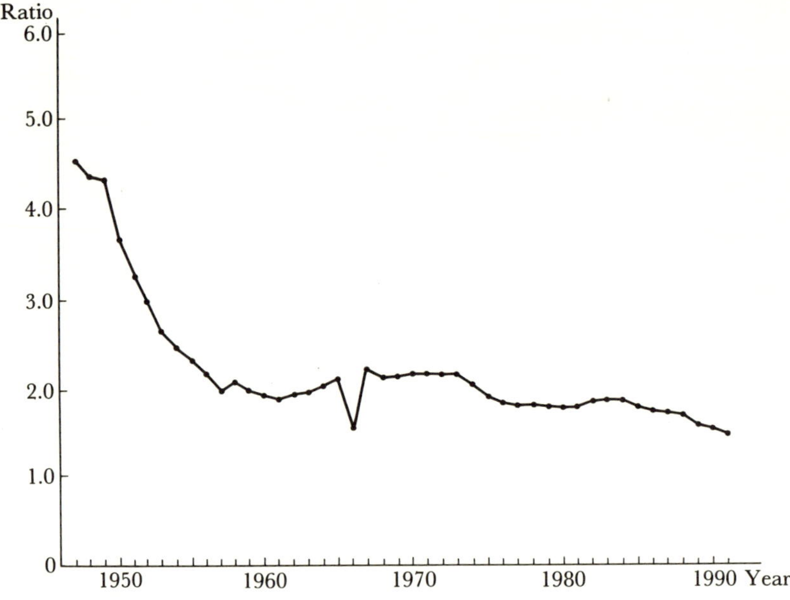

Figure 7.1   Total fertility rate

Source: Ministry of Health and Welfare Population Problems Research Institute, annual Dynamic Population Statistics.

Note: The total fertility rate is the aggregate birthrate among women of all ages for a particular year.

ture population, issued by the Population Problems Research Institute at the Ministry of Health and Welfare, the overall individual birthrate will continue to decline for the next few years, then bottom out and start slowly to rise again. The forecast is shown in Figure 7.2.

The study gives three different estimates, high, median, and low. The median scenario has the total fertility rate declining up to around 1995, then slowly recovering, to reach 1.78 by 2010, after which it continues to rise until it stabilizes at a level of around 1.85.

The sudden fall in the birthrate after 1985 seems to have been brought about largely by cost factors such as the rise in housing costs due to spiralling land prices, the rise in childcare and education costs, and the rise in "opportunity costs"—i.e., the rising cost of lost earnings to mothers whose childcare commitments prevent them from

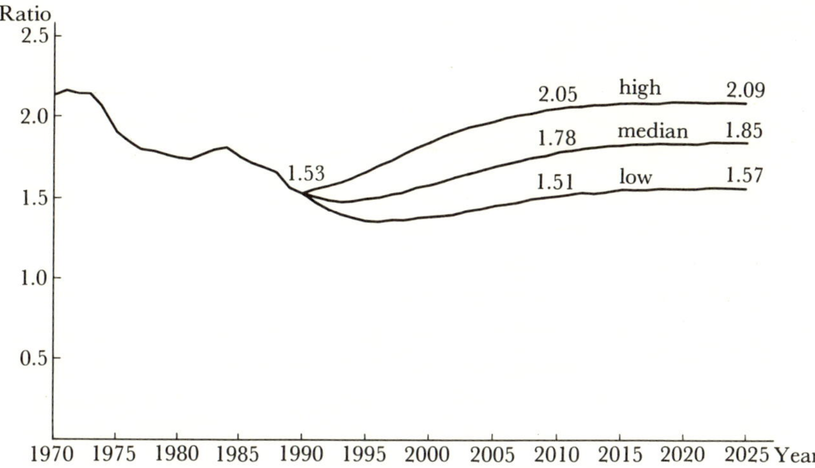

Figure 7.2   Trends in total fertility rate

Source: Ministry of Health and Welfare Population Problems Research Institute, "Estimates of Japan's Future Population" (provisional estimate as of June 1991).

working. While these costs have risen in all parts of the country in recent years, they have risen particularly steeply in the major cities. And the overall individual birthrate does in fact show a particularly sharp decline in urban regions. It seems unlikely that the next few years will see any great reduction in these costs, in which case there will probably be no rapid recovery in the birthrate.

Declining Population Is Not a Problem in Itself
In some quarters, the long-term trend toward a decline in the population has been greeted with some apprehension, so let us briefly analyze what such a decline would mean.

The decline in the population will bring with it an aging of the population structure, and there are fears that the rapid aging of the population will make it difficult for Japan to keep up pension payments and lead to a reduction in the investment capacity of the economy due to a fall in the savings rate. The decline in vitality spelled by the contraction and aging of the labor force, it is argued, will weaken productivity and lead to a decline in the power of the nation.

This argument certainly holds good for the transitional period while the population is in the process of aging. But the aging process is expected to peak in the first half of the 21st century. This should be followed by a period of stability, after which the population is expected to grow slightly younger. While the aging process is still underway, the pension system will be somewhat destabilized by the rapid shift in the balance between contributors to pension funds and their beneficiaries, but once the process has played itself out and the population recovers its stability, this balance should be restored.

There has also been some conjecture that the aging of the population will lead to a decline in the savings rate, but with the underlying surplus in the trade balance expected to continue for some time, there is likely to be more overseas investment, leading to a structural change over the long term whereby domestic savings, which have been declining throughout the Japanese economy, will be augmented by earnings from overseas assets. Hence the decline in the savings rate may not pose such a serious problem for the economy after all.

There are probably grounds for concern that a reduction in the size of the overall population will lead to a decline in national power, but this view is really a hangover from the 19th century when policies were dictated by national supremacism. National power really depends less on the size of the population than on the living standards of each individual citizen. A smaller population does not by itself constitute a problem; indeed it promises a higher rate of per-capita land and capital ownership and higher standards of living. The long-term decline in the Japanese population does not, therefore, provide grounds for justifying the introduction of foreign labor.

Decline in the Labor Force Centers on Younger Workers

The Ministry of Health and Welfare has come up with various estimates of the size of the future workforce based on its population estimates. The Ministry estimates that the total population will continue to rise very slowly at an annual rate of approximately 0.3% until the year 2000, after which the rate of increase will slow further. It expects the population to peak at 129 million in 2010, then start to decline at an annual rate of about 0.2%.

Given this dynamic, we can predict that the productive population between the ages of 15 and 64 will peak at 87 million by 1995 at the earliest, then start to decline, initially by 0.2% a year until 2000, then rather faster, by 0.6% a year until 2010, then slightly faster again, by 0.7% a year until 2020.

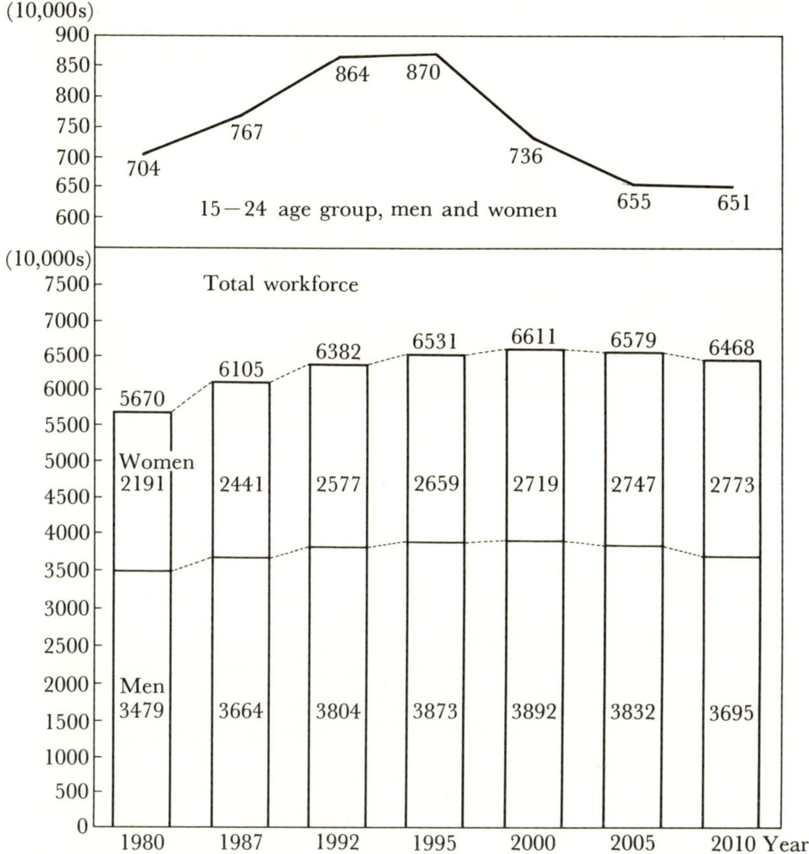

Figure 7.3   Estimates of future workforce

Source: Economic Council, Year 2010 Committee, "Report of the Subcommittee on Industry and the Economy," June 1991, p. 44.

Note: Data for 1980 and 1987 are from Management and Coordination Agency, "Labor Survey," and data for 1992 are from Economic Council, "Report of Committee on National Life" (April 1988). Data for 1995 and after, and those for the 15–24 age group, are estimates by the Planning Bureau of the Economic Planning Agency.

The labor force is defined as that sector of the population which is of productive age, and which has the will and ability to work, excluding students and full-time housewives. This is the workforce that provides the basis for industrial activity, and Figure 7.3 shows projected trends in the size of the labor force based on the above population estimates.

It is estimated that the total labor force will continue to expand gradually up to the year 2000, when it will peak at 66.11 million. It is then expected to decline, falling to 65.79 million by 2005, and to 64.68 million by 2010. Due to the decline in the birthrate up to now, the younger sections of the labor force will contract at a faster rate. The 15–24 age-group is expected to peak at 8.7 million in 1995, then decline rapidly to 7.36 million by 2000, and 6.55 million by 2005, down by more than two million from its peak.

Fears of a Labor Shortage

With the total labor force predicted to decrease over the long term and the size of the young workforce expected to decline particularly sharply, fears have naturally grown that there may not be sufficient labor to sustain industrial activity in the future.

These concerns have led several government agencies and private research institutes to carry out studies of future labor supply and demand. The estimate shown in Figure 7.3 was made by the Economic Planning Agency. The various estimates of future labor supply differ greatly, however, according to their assumptions of the labor force participation ratios for each age-sex group in the working population. The Ministry of Labor has published one preliminary study, based on the assumption that these proportions will remain the same as they were in 1990, which concludes that Japan will face labor shortages of 2.5 million in 2000, 5.5 million in 2005, and 9.1 million by 2010.[1] If, on the other hand, we assume a large increase in the proportion of women in the labor force, calculations based on the same population estimates point instead to a slight oversupply of labor, and suggest that it will take until the year 2010 for a labor shortage of just 1.8 million to emerge.[2]

The balance in labor supply and demand is influenced by so many such factors on both the supply and the demand sides that it is impossible to come up with an authoritative estimate. Demand is influenced by long-term prospects for growth in the national economy, increases in productivity, and changes in the industrial structure based on changes in the demand structure of the economy and changes in the structure of technology. Supply is influenced by trends in people's job preferences and by changes in the sex and age composition of the labor force, which are affected by population dynamics and trends in higher education and retirement.

Taking all these factors into account, we can to some extent predict

Table 7.1   Estimates of Labor Supply and Demand Balance by Industry

(Unit: 1,000 people)

	Total Men & Women		Men		Women	
	1995	2000	1995	2000	1995	2000
Industry total	−1329	−1250	−476	−721	−854	−529
Agriculture, forestry and fisheries	−74	−8	71	84	−145	−91
Mining	−13	−10	−12	−10	−1	−0
Construction	122	85	115	78	7	7
Machinery-related manufacturing	−20	171	−297	−340	277	512
Other manufacturing	111	−118	−324	−638	435	520
Electricity, gas, heating supply and water supply	−17	−21	−11	−15	−6	−6
Wholesale, retail and restaurant	−1260	−1377	−333	−392	−927	−984
Finance, insurance and real estate	−211	−258	−8	−18	−203	−240
Transport and communications	−47	253	21	279	−68	−26
Service	79	33	302	252	−223	−219

Source: Research Group on How Employment Policy Should Respond to Changes in the Labor Supply, "Towards the Realization of a People-Oriented Employment System for the 21st Century" (January 1991), p. 116.

Notes: (1) Figures represent labor supply in terms of numbers of employees, and are estimates provided by the above research institute.

(2) "Machinery-related manufacturing" includes metal products, general machinery, precision machinery, electrical equipment, and transportation equipment.

labor supply and demand by industry and type of job, though not to any great degree of accuracy. Tables 7.1 and 7.2 present forecasts of labor supply and demand by sector. They show that significant gaps may open up between different industries and types of job.

The wholesaling, retailing, restaurant, finance, insurance, and real estate industries will tend to have a surplus of labor supply, while

Table 7.2   Estimates of Labor Supply and Demand Balance by Type of Employment

(Unit: 1,000 people)

	Total Men & Women		Men		Women	
	1995	2000	1995	2000	1995	2000
Total for all types of employment	−1329	−1250	−476	−721	−854	−529
Specialist and technical	552	793	590	747	−38	46
Management	−1000	−1487	−837	−1253	−163	−234
Clerical	−435	35	784	1405	−1219	−1370
Sales	−37	−248	435	301	−472	−550
Agricultural, forestry and fisheries	−35	38	103	116	−138	−78
Mining	−39	−32	−38	−31	−1	−1
Transport and communications	−113	111	2	229	−115	−118
Skilled labor factory work and manual labor	216	72	−1192	−1747	1408	1819
Security and misc. services	−435	−530	−226	−356	−209	−174

Source: See Table 7.1.

Note: Figures represent labor supply in terms of numbers of employees, and are estimates.

construction, manufacturing, and transportation will suffer a growing labor shortage. Meanwhile, the tables show a clear trend toward an oversupply of labor for management-type white collar jobs, but a shortage of labor for specialist and technical jobs like engineering, as well as for blue-collar production-site jobs like technical and factory work and manual labor.

Will There Really Be a Labor Shortage?
Such estimates of future labor supply are inevitably based on certain assumptions. I have done this sort of analysis myself a number of

times and, while it is well known how carefully such studies are conducted, it must also be acknowledged that they have severe limitations.[3]

As we have seen, studies of this kind rely on the predicted or hypothetical values of a number of basic variables, and any change in these values strongly influences their results. Hence their conclusions are a useful indication of certain possibilities, but nothing more.

Another more substantial limitation of these analyses is that they presuppose the current economic structure, and contemporary business and household patterns of behavior and choices. In the real economy, however, there is a constant dynamic by which people's patterns of thought and behavior shift in response to changes in environmental conditions, and this in turn influences the technological and economic structure. The type of study we have looked at cannot very well presuppose or incorporate such changes, so they inevitably fall short as accurate forecasts of what will occur.

The question of whether there will actually be a labor shortage is a good illustration of these shortcomings. Studies of this kind can estimate the supply and demand gap based on today's economic structure, but the actual economy is unlikely to behave so predictably. In the final analysis, there will probably not be a labor shortage.

The reason is that the economy is a self-regulating system. Any relative decline in labor supply over demand is compensated for by a rise in the price of labor, i.e., wage rates. And rising wage rates force employers to increase productivity (either by technical innovation or by rationalization), order from overseas or move production abroad, or else go out of business. With higher wages, this results in a change in the technological and economic structure, and labor supply and demand find a new balance.

The introduction of foreign labor can be thought of as one method of ordering from overseas, but as such it is only one of several options, and there are no grounds for asserting that the Japanese economy would face an absolute labor shortage without foreign labor. On the contrary, if no foreign labor were introduced, this would exert pressure on the supply and demand balance, which would act to raise wage levels for a labor force in relatively short supply. The economy as a whole would then establish a new equilibrium through further technical innovation and changes in the economic structure, and this would prevent any absolute shortage of labor from arising.

It is also feared that a labor shortage could lead to a slowdown in economic growth, but we cannot be sure that this is what would really happen. It does seem a likely outcome if we base our calculations on the premise of existing economic structure and the present technological level. If we simply assume a fixed rate of increase in productivity over the long run, then obviously the economy will grow more slowly when the labor force is growing slowly than when it is growing at a faster rate.

In the real economy, however, there can be large fluctuations in the rate of increase in productivity. Viewed with hindsight, the past experience both of Japan and of other nations shows that major changes do in fact occur. There have been times when productivity has risen greatly despite a low rate of increase in the labor force, and the reverse has also been true. So the fact that estimates of Japan's future labor force predict that it will grow more slowly or even contract in absolute terms does not necessarily preclude the possibility of an enormous increase in productivity, through technological innovation or some other means, which would cancel out the decline.

Scope for Reform and Improved Efficiency in the Economic Structure
So far we have considered the possibility of changes in the economic structure and higher productivity from a rather abstract standpoint; but let us now look at the Japanese economy from the point of view of more concrete realities.

The Japanese economy is often said to be founded on trade. The export industries earn foreign exchange through exports, and foreign exchange earnings are used to import food, raw materials, and energy. But when we look at the economy from the point of view of the structure of employment, we find that only a very small proportion of the total workforce is employed in the export-related industries, while the great majority is engaged in the domestic service industries and in production for the domestic market. We can broadly define the former types of industry as the tradable goods sector, and the latter as the sector of non-tradable goods.

Table 7.3 shows Japan's employment structure by industry. The table gives figures for both the actual past structure and the predicted future structure of employment. Let us look at 1995, for example, when the total size of the workforce is predicted to be approximately

Table 7.3 Trends and Future Estimated Numbers of Workers by Industry

(Unit: 10,000 people)

	1985	1989	1995	2000	2005	2010
Industry total	5807	6128	6449	6607	6637	6585
Primary industries	509	463	365	305	241	174
Agriculture, forestry and fisheries	509	463	365	305	241	174
Secondary industries	1992	2069	2176	2200	2155	2140
Mining	9	7	7	7	7	7
Manufacturing industry (except machinery)	834	840	849	850	795	763
Machinery	619	644	713	715	701	700
Construction	530	578	607	628	652	670
Tertiary industries	3283	3566	3908	4102	4241	4271
Electricity, gas, heating, and water-supply	33	30	31	31	31	31
Wholesale, retail and restaurant	1318	1400	1533	1560	1592	1596
Finance, insurance and real estate	217	243	245	259	263	259
Transport and communications	343	368	376	386	384	321
Service industries	1372	1525	1723	1866	1971	2064

Source: Mitsubishi General Research Institute, "A Survey of Cutbacks in the Labor Supply and Employment and the Economy" (January 1991).

Note: Data for 1985 and 1989 are from Management and Coordination Agency, Statistics Bureau, "Survey of Labor." Data for 1990 and after are estimates based on the results of this survey.

64.5 million. Out of this total, the trade sector will account for about half of those employed in manufacturing, centering on the machinery industry, but only a very small proportion of those employed in various other industries. This segment of the workforce will probably employ about 10 million people in all.

This means there will be more than 54 million people employed in other sectors of industry, practically all of them in the non-tradable goods sector. There will probably be about 6 million people employed in construction, 15 million in the wholesale, retail, and restaurant industries, 17 million in the service industries, 3.7 million in transportation and communications, and 2.4 million in finance, insurance, and real estate.

The employment structure has gradually changed in quantitative terms since 1980, but the change is not particularly marked. And predictions of future trends do not foresee any dramatic change in the structure between now and 2010. But since the second half of the 1980s there have been great changes in the relative levels of productivity of the tradable and the non-tradable goods and services sectors. While the productivity of the tradable goods sector has grown enormously, that in non-tradable goods and services has grown rather slowly.

These changes are faithfully reflected in trends in prices and real purchasing power since the mid-1980s. In the second half of the 1980s there was a huge appreciation in the value of the yen, provoked by the Plaza Accord of 1985. This should have greatly reduced the prices of Japan's imports, and worked substantially to raise the real purchasing power of the Japanese currency by reducing domestic prices overall, but in fact the real purchasing power of the yen rose only slightly compared with the enormous rise in the exchange rate.

The main reason was that Japan's productivity in the non-tradable goods and services sector rose relatively little. Industries in this sector, as we have seen, employ very large numbers of people and provide goods and services that are closely connected to people's everyday lives. Productivity in these industries rose very little, and because Japan has numerous regulations that protect jobs in such industries, the benefits of the huge appreciation of the yen were not passed back to the Japanese consumer.

This illustrates something which has an extremely important bearing on the foreign labor question, namely that there is still a great deal of scope for increased productivity in the sector of non-tradable goods and services, which absorbs such enormous quantities of labor. If this sector were to achieve a much higher level of productivity commensurate with the present exchange rate of the yen, it would no longer need to employ a workforce as large as 50 million. It could achieve the same level of production with a substantially smaller labor force. If it increased labor productivity by an average 30%, for example, it would probably find itself with a labor surplus of between 10 and 15 million people.[4]

If this surplus were absorbed by the sectors of industry which are short of labor, the rationale for depending on foreign labor would collapse completely.

Rationalizing and modernizing to raise productivity, changing jobs, or breaking into a new business tend to be hard on all concerned. It is surely more humane to try and avoid such upheavals if at all possible, since they involve major changes in people's lifestyles and work patterns. People are only willing to put up with this sort of hardship and take on the task of reforming their businesses when they are either threatened by tough competition or when the very survival of the business is at stake. The most effective way to encourage such reform and increase productivity, then, is by liberalizing and opening up markets. Opening markets to the outside world not only fosters international coexistence and raises living standards by lowering prices, but also, through rationalization and modernization strengthens the foundation for the survival of domestic industry.

2. The Rationalization and Modernization of Domestic Industry and the Utilization of Labor

Policies for Rationalizing and Modernizing Domestic Industry

I have suggested that there is ample scope for increased efficiency in the non-tradable goods and services sector. We will now focus on a few major industries and suggest some rather more concrete policies for rationalizing and modernizing.

Let us take agriculture first. The industry employs about 4 million people, of whom about 700,000 are engaged in farming full-time, while the remainder have other jobs and farm as a sideline. Part-time farmers can be classified as either those for whom farming is the main source of income or those whose farming income is secondary. More or less half of part-time farmers fall into each category.

The major difficulty now confronting Japanese agriculture is the falloff in the growth of labor productivity. Future prospects for the industry are bleak: the farming population is aging, fewer and fewer farmers' children are interested in remaining on the land, and those that do have difficulty finding marriage partners.

If these difficulties are to be overcome, Japan will have to greatly increase agricultural productivity. And probably the most effective strategy for increasing productivity will be to modernize farm management and increase land-intensiveness so as to take advantage of the economies of scale.

Modernizing farm management will mean fostering full-time farmers with proper management skills. If such farmers are allowed to consolidate their land, they will benefit from the economies of scale, and productivity should rise greatly. More land-intensive farms could be created if part-time farmers were to lease their land to full-time farmers for rent. The full-time farmers would be able to afford to rent the land with a portion of the profits that would accrue from increased productivity on larger farms.

To promote such a strategy, Japan will have to revise the laws covering agriculture; liberalize, mobilize, and concentrate the ownership of farmland; and create opportunities for new people wishing to take up farming, other than those taking over family farms from their parents. Implementing a series of such reforms would enormously modernize farm management and increase productivity. The overall number of people employed in agriculture would decline greatly, but the reforms would probably alleviate the shortage of farm labor and the lack of people prepared to continue working family farms.

Now let us look at construction. This is a very large industry, employing 6 million people, and it has a peculiar and rather complex structure, being made up of a small number of giant corporations and an enormously large number of very small contractors. Because the building trade is basically one that produces to order, production efficiency is low. But there is plenty of scope for improving productivity in the industry through the standardization of building specifications and materials, mechanization, and the use of robots.[5]

Another problem is that, since the construction industry is very vulnerable to fluctuations in the economy, it tends to suffer severe labor shortages when the economy is doing well, whereas working conditions can easily deteriorate in times of recession, and the industry is perpetually plagued by difficulties in the training and commitment of workers.[6]

The best way to overcome these difficulties would be to stabilize and modernize working conditions in the industry, stabilize incomes, improve the working environment, and radically improve access to jobs and training.[7] Such a policy could easily be effected by the strategic use of construction industry employment insurance funds and by individual construction companies making a concerted effort to modernize their businesses. Once the industry has modernized and raised productivity, it should be able to maintain production with a much smaller number of well-qualified permanent employees.

Next, let us take a brief look at the modernization of the distribution and service industries. Like the construction industry, the distribution industry is complex in structure and made up of an enormous number of small companies with low productivity, whose existence is a major obstacle to the modernization of the industry. These small businesses are now undergoing a shakeup, brought on by labor shortages, increased costs incurred by reduced working hours, and a shortage of younger people willing to carry on family businesses. But there is considerable opportunity for rationalization and modernization through, for instance, an aggressive policy of joint management.

Small businesses in the service industries face similar difficulties, but the main problem here is how to set fair prices for services in the Japanese market. If prices were more subject to market forces, firms offering high-quality services could expand greatly, while those which did not make the grade would be weeded out. If the non-tradable goods and services sector can be rationalized and modernized in this way, inefficient, low value-added distribution and service firms and those whose services are of poorer quality will disappear, while productivity will rise throughout the sector, and there should be a large reduction in the amount of labor it absorbs.

The Effective Use of Human Resources
Japanese firms are frequently said to practise "humanist" management, but in fact they do not always utilize their human resources in the most effective way. The gap between wage costs and labor productivity has become a particularly serious structural problem since the large appreciation of the yen in the mid-1980s.

While the rise in the exchange value of the yen enormously raised Japanese wage costs internationally, Japanese industries did not make up for the change by utilizing labor more efficiently. International wage costs were greatly inflated; yet, since real domestic wages were stable, industry continued to implement traditional employment and personnel policies unchanged. The fact that so many companies have failed to make proper use of their human resources, whose efficiency should have been greatly improved to compensate for the change in the exchange rate, has widened the gap between wage costs and labor productivity, pressured business, and reduced its efficiency.

There is plenty of scope for improvement in the use of human resources, but let us look at just a few examples. First, employees' time could be used more effectively. Many adjustments and improvements could be made by investing in equipment modernization, improving labor productivity, reorganizing work schedules, improving the efficiency of meetings, improving management methods, reforming pay systems through annual fixed salaries for discretionary work, and making more effective use of information support systems.

Another area where efficiency could be improved is in the use of women and older workers. Women must be allocated more responsible work, so as to improve their skills, and personnel policy must be reviewed to enable women to meet their home commitments without having to give up their jobs, so that their abilities can be utilized over a much longer term.

Another way firms can improve efficiency is by making more use of "flow-type" employment. Both technology and demand are undergoing dramatic changes, while on the labor supply side a much wider variety of people, including women, middle-aged and older people, and people with special abilities, are taking on an increasingly large role in the workforce. Businesses should try to make effective use of the whole of this valuable and diverse labor force, taking on temporary workers, whose market value lies in their instant usability, as well as long-term permanent employees.

These are just a few examples, but in other ways too, as labor becomes a scarcer commodity, businesses will have to adopt a strategy of utilizing their human resources in a more effective manner.

3. Institutional Reform for More Open Organizations and a More Open Society

Throughout this book so far the discussion of foreign workers has focussed almost exclusively on unregistered workers, but foreign workers of course also include people with specialist skills and knowledge.[8]

As we saw in Chapter 3, under the current Immigration Control Law, these people suffer few legal or institutional problems with regard to immigration or employment. They can enter the country legally to work, and it is easier to get permission to work in Japan than in many other countries. This does not mean, however, that such people necessarily find it easy to work in Japanese companies or feel comfortable in Japanese society. Such difficulties obviously constitute a problem for them, but it also represents a loss to Japanese society. Not only does it mean Japanese companies are unable to engage capable individuals from abroad and fully utilize their abilities; it also deprives society of the fresh stimulus of talented people from other cultures, and creates the impression overseas that Japan is a closed society. I would like now to focus on two aspects of this problem in particular.

Clarifying Information within Organizations

One of the major difficulties foreigners face when working in a Japanese company is their inability to feel at home in the organization and get "inside" it.

Japanese companies do not make any particular distinctions or discriminate against foreigners. Talented foreign workers find the rules of the workplace, salaries, and qualifications for promotion are all quite clearly set out, and they generally have no difficulty communicating with their colleagues, at least on the level of language. Yet they are still not quite able to fit in. One often hears of foreign employees in Japanese firms who say they are unable really to feel that they are members of the company. They have no complaints over their salary, neither are they handicapped by the difficulty of the language, yet they say they are conscious of an invisible barrier that prevents them ever being anything other than foreigners.

Individual foreigners no doubt differ in the degree to which they feel this sense of alienation, but their experience points to a deep problem shared by all Japanese companies and organizations. The problem can be characterized by a lack of transparency in information. Information does not serve effectively as a tool of communication. Language is used, but the meaning of the words plays only a very limited role in enabling mutual understanding.

This problem is not confined to communication between Japanese and foreigners. It happens every day between Japanese as well. In Japanese organizations, clear communication cannot be fully achieved through verbal information alone. All sorts of elements other than language come into play. And because so many intangible elements interpose, the information exchanged within organizations comes to have rather a complex overall structure, and inevitably comes to lack transparency. The ultimate way of sharing this ambiguous type of information is to accumulate shared experience among the people involved through a long process of working together.

The more experience of communication they have, and the more deeply shared it is, the less need people have to communicate their intentions to others clearly by means of language. In extreme cases it becomes possible to communicate by signs and gestures without recourse to language at all, and to know what people are thinking just by watching them closely. Japanese organizations and society have always stressed the importance of fostering this kind of tacit understanding. Most Japanese are brought up in the same environment from infancy, go to the same schools and receive the same kind of education, enter similar kinds of companies, and work with colleagues who are very similar to themselves. Furthermore, they work together all the time during the work week, often in a large room in full view of each other; and on public holidays and during their time off they often continue to associate with workplace colleagues. And quite a large number of people live in company housing, so they tend to share the same experiences even in their family life.

Living and working within the structure of Japanese organizations and corporate society, where shared experience is repeated and reinforced all the time, people forget even to explain things clearly and express their thoughts systematically, which is the very first step in communication.

People in homogeneous groups where everyone possesses the same experience can no doubt communicate effectively by means of astonishingly rudimentary signals and wordless gestures, but these have scarcely any meaning at all for people who do not share that experience. Hence, the problem of communication gaps is not confined to relations between Japanese and foreigners. Japanese who lack a common experience frequently fail to communicate properly as well.

Some good examples of this are the gap between male and female employees in Japanese companies, the gaps between different companies and groups of companies, and the gap between people graduating from different schools. It is not in the least surprising therefore that foreign employees, even though fluent in Japanese, feel unable to get close to their colleagues in Japanese companies.

This pattern in organizations and society is an enormous obstacle to Japan's future development. Organizations and information systems of this kind, which find it difficult to tolerate diversity, not only constitute an internal barrier to the internationalization of Japanese companies, but suffocate any stimulus that might be sparked by the collision of diverse elements, and hinder the development of creativity in organizations.

What can be done to correct this defect that seems to pervade Japanese corporate organizations? One remedy would be to clarify and objectify as far as possible the shared information that is exchanged within them. Another might be to incorporate as many diverse elements into the organization as possible. The introduction of skilled foreign workers could be a very powerful strategy for reforming the nature of Japanese organizations and developing creativity. It would benefit not only companies which are engaged in production but also organizations like universities and research institutions that must pursue the development of intellectual creativity.

Building a System That Takes Diversity for Granted

Japanese organizations, and society as a whole, share a basic, characteristic flaw. They fail to accept the premise that diversity exists, and are constructed in ways that ignore it. Since, as we have seen, Japanese organizations are designed to include only homogeneous groups, the core groups of organizations find them very comfortable, while groups which are outside of the nucleus of the organization find themselves in a rather uncomfortable and uneasy environment where nothing is quite what it seems.[9]

The core group of an organization is typically made up of university-graduate, white-collar, full-time male employees. These people come from prestigious universities, are well schooled in the inner workings of the organization, have a firm foothold on the ladder of promotion, and possess common corporate goals and managerial values. By contrast, the corporate organization is not geared to the needs of women, people with lower levels of education, or temporary employees. The company neither sees the problems these people face from their angle nor makes enough of an attempt to solve them. Foreign employees are also outsiders in the sense that they are heterogeneous to the core group of the corporation.

Japanese companies must first accept that their organizations do in fact contain a diversity of people from many different backgrounds.

Then they must put themselves in these people's shoes, come to grips with the inherent problems they face, and try to understand their aspirations. Companies should deal with all the various groups and individuals even-handedly, and try to solve their problems on the basis of fair rules and easily understood procedures.

In doing this, they must encourage employees from diverse backgrounds to feel proud of the company and think of it as "theirs." Foreign employees should not be made to think of their firm as a "Japanese company" or feel themselves to be outsiders. Employees must not be made to feel that the company belongs to the elite group at its core, and that everybody else is excluded. In a company that employs foreigners, all the diverse members of the company should be able to feel that the company belongs to them.

In society at large, however, there is an even more fundamental problem to overcome, which is that the basic framework of Japanese society is simply not designed on the premise that foreigners exist.[10]

It is true that universal equality under the law is enshrined in Article 14 of the current Japanese constitution. This is a fundamental principle applied without regard to people's nationality or origin. For foreigners actually living and working in Japanese society, however, there is hardly any concrete legislative framework that guarantees them equal treatment with Japanese.

For people discriminated against in housing, or in their everyday lives, purely on the grounds that they are foreigners, there is hardly any legal recourse. And foreigners face many additional problems as well. Society makes little allowance for the fact that foreigners may have difficulty meeting conditions that are easily fulfilled by Japanese. They are frequently required to supply guarantors, for example, before they can engage in business activities; they are often refused employment just because they are foreigners; some jobs require qualifications that they cannot possibly obtain; and there are many aspects of economic activity that foreigners simply cannot participate in.

In addition, as symbolized by the inadequacy of Japanese language learning facilities and the difficulty of access to housing, Japan lacks many of the facilities and systems foreigners need to settle comfortably into Japanese society.

It should be a major priority for Japan's future development to accept foreigners and forge new values out of the exchange and stimulation their presence will encourage. Yet one has to say that Japan still lags far behind in creating the legal, institutional, and social conditions that would make this possible.

Notes

[1] Ministry of Labor estimate, *Nihon Keizai Shimbun* article, June 19, 1990, morning edition.

[2] Ibid.

[3] Haruo Shimada, Kazuyoshi Koshiro, and Masahiko Shimizu, "Changes in the Employment Structure and Lifetime Education," General Research and Development Organization, 1980. Haruo Shimada, *Labor Economics* (Iwanami Shoten, 1986), chapter 7.

[4] Masao Yokomizo, "Japan Has a Surplus Workforce of 14 Million," *Economist*, March 6, 1990.

[5] The general construction companies can and should play a leading role in the modernization of the construction industry and the improvement of productivity. Shoji Sasaki, *Construction Labor and Foreigners* (Taisei Shuppansha, January 1991).

[6] Tomio Higuchi, "Comparative Employment Trends in the Construction and Manufacturing Industries," in Labor Market Research Committee, *Changes in the Economic Structure and the Labor Market* (Statistical Research Group, August 1991).

[7] The Central Construction Industry Council's Special Committee on Personnel (chair, Takafusa Nakamura) advocates a comprehensive policy to tackle the problem of securing personnel, and stresses in particular the reduction of working hours, stabilization of incomes, improvement of working conditions and the working environment, better organization and improvement of job access, personnel training, and a thorough evaluation of businesses. "The Future of the Construction Industry in Response to New Socioeconomic Conditions: Securing Personnel in the Construction Industry," Central Construction Industry Council, February 1993.

[8] Many firms cite the stimulus of different ideas as one advantage of employing specialist foreign workers. Japan Association of Overseas Corporations, "Survey of the Employment of Specialist Foreign Workers," February 1988. There are many cases where firms employing specialist foreign workers strongly endorse the advantages of the practice. Ministry of Labor, "Case Studies of Foreign Worker Employment Management," July 1990.

[9] Jackson N. Huddleston (Masumi Matsumura and Satoshi Watanabe, trans.), *Gaijin Company: Hints for Managing a Business in Japan* (Simul Press, 1993), is a very interesting study that deals frankly with the various internal and external problems faced by foreign companies operating in Japan.

[10] In employing specialist foreign workers, many firms cite institutional obstacles such as residence status, employment regulations, part-time contracts, and the health and welfare system based on the premise of lifetime employment. Japan Association of Overseas Corporations, "Survey of the Employment of Specialist Foreign Workers," February 1988.

8
What Kind of Nation Do We Want to Be?

The problem of foreign workers is both an old problem and a new one for many nations around the world. It has been experienced by almost all advanced nations, in all parts of the world, throughout history.

The more advanced nations have always had relatively higher income levels and an excess of labor demand over supply. Labor shortages have generally centered on relatively low-paying, unskilled jobs. And nations have customarily compensated for bottlenecks in the labor supply by introducing labor from abroad.

In recent years, the situation has been complicated by greatly increased international movements of population and labor. The phenomenal spread of information through the mass media and other channels, and great strides in transport and communications technology, have made it much easier for people to cross national borders, and they have done so with increasing frequency. In addition to this, the economic collapse of the Soviet Union and the other communist nations since the late 1980s, and growing political unrest in the Middle East, Africa, and Indochina, have caused floods of political and economic refugees to pour across national borders into neighboring countries and regions.

Japan has also been swept up in a wave of changes both at home and abroad. Its economy is beginning to exhibit the typical features of a mature industrialized economy. With economic growth and higher income levels, the rate of increase in the population has slowed, and the nation now faces an absolute decline in the labor supply, particularly the supply of younger workers. The balance of labor supply and demand does fluctuate in response to cyclical changes in the economy, but there is no doubt that Japan's underlying labor shortage will grow more severe over the long term.

As I have repeatedly indicated, this trend does not immediately presage an absolute shortage of labor. Indeed no absolute labor shortage can arise so long as market forces continue to operate, because labor demand and supply are always adjusted on the basis of changes in wages and prices, or by technological innovation. Of course such structural changes are not made easily, but tend to involve frictions, costs, and hardships. So the larger and more sudden the changes required, the more strongly people will resist them, in a bid to avoid these effects. And the more strongly people resist self-reform, the more they will tend to resort to foreign labor as the easiest way to make up for labor shortages. This is exactly the process that Japan is caught up in today.

Seen from the outside, Japan seems an extremely attractive place to work, with its high income levels and abundant work opportunities. Many foreign workers have already found their way into the Japanese labor market, and are playing a far from insignificant role in supporting Japan's economy. While unskilled foreign workers are barred in principle from entering the country to work, in actual fact large numbers are working illegally, and there appears to be a well-established network helping them to get into the country and to find jobs.

So people within the country have a strong economic incentive to introduce foreign labor to alleviate the bottleneck in labor supply, while people outside the country have a strong incentive to participate in the Japanese labor market due to the attraction of high earnings. So long as these two factors conspire to encourage it, then, Japan is bound to see a gradual increase in the influx of foreign labor.

While the trend may seem economically inevitable, however, it is bound to create problems on the social front. There are grounds for concern that an influx of foreign workers into Japanese society, depending on how it occurs, could give rise to discrimination, a dual structure in society, or a social backlash, while Japanese society may simply be unable to absorb them. It is also likely to throw up a range of new problems for Japan's legal and other social systems, and could lead to clashes of customs, values, and cultures, as Japanese are called upon to coexist with people from very different backgrounds.

The foreign worker problem is also likely to call into question Japan's position in the world community. It is undeniable that Japan has forged ahead of the world, and even of the other industrialized countries, in terms of economic and income opportunities, and yet it still protects its homogeneity on the human level, and plainly gives the outside world the impression that it is a closed society.

A world with this negative image will see Japan's response to the foreign worker problem as an important test case of whether or not it has any intention or possibility of changing. One way Japan could change would be to bow to the economic incentive and continue to accept more and more foreign labor. But there is a danger that continuing to accept increasing numbers of foreign workers without making appropriate institutional and social arrangements, in terms of legal, social, and policy measures, will deepen resistance, friction, and discrimination against foreigners, and make it even more difficult to deal with the situation effectively. If, on the other hand, Japan does manage to implement the necessary policy, legal, and social measures in a form that enables foreign workers to be absorbed smoothly, this implies a considerable change for Japan in a different sense.

Japan's response to the problem also calls into question its response to the world population problem. Japan and most of the other industrialized countries have low birthrates, and their populations are set to decline over the long term. Developing regions like South Asia and Africa, by contrast, still have high birthrates, and the 21st century will see significant changes in the relative distribution of population between the industrialized nations and the rest of the world. As we saw in Chapter 6, the industrialized countries will account for a smaller proportion of world population, while the developing countries come to make up the overwhelming majority. People in the industrialized countries will maintain high levels of income and a high standard of living, but the further increase in the populations of those regions that make up the overwhelming bulk of the world's population will probably exacerbate their already widespread problems of poverty and environmental degradation.

How will—or, indeed, should—Japan, as a maturing industrialized nation, respond to problems brought on by these movements in the world population? In this concluding chapter, I would like to present four different potential scenarios for Japan's future. Based on these scenarios, I will then give my own view as to the course Japan would be best advised to take.

The Discriminatory Nation Scenario

The first scenario that comes to mind is that of Japan as a discriminatory nation: foreign workers continue to pour into the country, most of them continue to work illegally, and some stay on and settle down. These people have difficulty speaking the language, they lack useful skills and training, and because their status and position are unstable, they tend to be shut out of Japanese society and discriminated against. Most of them form an underclass of their own, and Japanese society comes to have a permanently two-tiered structure.

How would such a Japan be seen by the outside world? The foreign worker problem is an intractable one for any country, and none of the industrialized countries, where incomes are relatively higher than in neighboring regions, are immune to illegal immigration by foreign workers. All these nations have encountered difficult social problems in dealing with foreign workers.

Many countries have acquired a dual or multilayered social structure that clearly discriminates against foreigners, immigrant groups, and people of other races. To take some of the most extreme cases, South Africa was until recently an international pariah for its openly racist apartheid policies, Kuwait's extremely discriminatory social policies treated native Kuwaitis differently from Palestinians and people of other races, and Yugoslavia has been torn apart by ethnic strife.

How would the rest of the world react if such problems were to develop in Japanese society and a discriminatory structure gradually became plain for all to see? In contrast to the ethnic and racial tensions in many smaller countries, problems in Japan are bound to be linked directly to its economic power and dominance of world markets. The image of Japan likely to be etched most vividly in the minds of people overseas is that of a nation that, not content with dominating world markets and reaping profits from all over the globe, discriminates against and exploits foreign workers at home.

And if this is the image that sticks in people's minds, one can easily imagine what damage it could do to Japan's foreign relations and the nation's future in international society.

The Closed-Door Scenario

Another scenario one can envisage is that of Japan as a closed nation. ("Closed" of course means closed to foreign labor, not totally shut off from the world.) It is argued that Japan could avoid the pitfalls of the first scenario by excluding foreign labor altogether.

Closing the country, however, is much more easily said than done. Even from a purely theoretical point of view, to stop the influx of unskilled foreign workers and still maintain the same level of economic activity would entail considerable structural reform in terms of labor force allocation, business activity, and the structure of industry.

Already there are probably at any one time as many as a million foreign workers employed in the Japanese labor market. This is still a very small number when set against the official statistic of Japan's total labor force, which is well over 64 million, but we should note that the majority are employed in the unskilled, "dirty, dangerous, and demanding" jobs that Japanese workers do not want to do. In other words, while their numbers may seem insignificant, if they were not available to do these jobs, or if they were eliminated from the workforce, the businesses and industries that have come to rely on them would no longer be able to function, and this would result in a severe bottleneck in the labor supply to those sectors.

Again, while there may appear to be a limited number of unskilled foreign workers employed in Japanese industry today, the Japanese economy's dependence on unskilled foreign labor can, based on present trends, be expected to increase markedly in future, due to the declining size of the Japanese labor force, particularly its younger sectors, and trends in the career choices and job preferences of young people brought up in an age of affluence. If Japan were to adopt a closed-door policy in spite of these trends, the current labor bottleneck would become very much larger and more serious.

If, given these realities, Japan still opted for the closed-door scenario, wages would escalate in the sectors that inevitably face labor shortages, and this would cause changes in the price structure. These sectors of industry are essential to people's everyday lives and economic activities, and if there were little price elasticity of demand, higher wages would be passed on to prices. If they were not, these sectors would have to undergo radical restructuring—switching their lines of business, transferring their operations overseas, rationalizing and introducing new technology—or else be forced to the wall.

I personally believe such a reform and rationalization, indeed modernization, of the domestic economic structure would be a good thing. But it would be a tough and unpalatable option for most employers. The closed-door scenario would force businesses to make the most strenuous efforts to reform themselves.

The Integration Scenario
The third scenario we will consider is that of integration. This would mean thinking of foreign workers as no different from Japanese, and accepting them into society on exactly the same terms as Japanese citizens. More exactly, since the Japanese do not always regard each

other as the same, it would mean a readiness to coexist with foreigners utterly without discrimination, letting them mix freely and meld into society, on the basis of their common humanity, regardless of any differences.

If foreigners could actually be integrated in this way, the foreign worker problem would disappear of itself. It would make no sense to distinguish oneself from someone doing the same work only on the basis of nationality. If Japanese and foreigners lived and worked together in a non-discriminatory atmosphere, there might still be labor problems, but there would no longer be any "foreign worker problem."

It is easy to envisage such an ideal society on the conceptual level, but it will be far less easy to put those ideas into practice. Treating foreigners exactly the same as Japanese would mean according them complete equality both in terms of the law and social systems and in terms of customs and popular attitudes. And in the real world, equality in either of these areas will not be at all easy to accomplish.

On the legal and social side, foreigners would have to be granted exactly the same rights and legal guarantees as Japanese citizens. In an abstract sense, people's rights to exist and their basic human rights are guaranteed under the constitution, but the nation would have to face up to the more concrete questions of whether it was prepared to grant foreigners identical rights to Japanese citizens under the labor and social security laws and give them equal treatment with regard to employment, housing, education, and voting rights. When we look at specific problems like granting foreigners full rights to unemployment insurance, medical treatment, and pensions, for instance, it is clear such questions would not be easy to resolve.

The problem of people's attitudes and social customs would be even more intractable. Even if foreigners achieved full equality with Japanese in all the legal areas mentioned above, and there were absolutely no institutional discrimination against them, it would be naive to imagine that social discrimination would just go away. Despite the official outlawing of job discrimination in Japan, it is proving difficult to put an end to discriminatory practices even among Japanese. And it appears to be equally difficult in other countries as well. It will always be difficult to eradicate habits of discrimination, whether on the grounds that someone is a foreigner or because they have not been fully accepted into some group within society.

Even more fundamental than discrimination in employment is discrimination in marriage and family relations. As I have already indicated, people's attitudes to marriage serve as a useful index of social discrimination. If someone is prepared to allow their own son or daughter to marry a foreigner, they must have basically overcome their prejudice. There can be no question of discrimination if you are prepared to have grandchildren of diverse ancestry, and are willing to bequeath to them the assets you have spent a lifetime accumulating.

If different races and peoples were mingled in this way it would eventually render meaningless any confrontation between ethnic nation-states, so in a sense a policy of integration could be seen as a powerful security strategy. Indeed, in a different sense, it might ultimately erode the raison d'être of the nation state itself.

Once foreigners of whatever origin were treated identically to Japanese, granted exactly the same rights, and fully assimilated into society, people might start wondering what it really meant to belong to a nation. But then they would start questioning what it was they had worked so hard for, payed their taxes for, educated their children for, and amassed fortunes for. They would wonder what all that effort had been for, when people who had not shared their history or made the same efforts as themselves could still claim the same rights.

The integration scenario inevitably raises these very basic questions. It is easy to talk about such a scenario, but it would be extremely difficult to bring it about.

The Sophisticated Discrimination Scenario
The final scenario we will consider is that of "sophisticated discrimination." In this scenario foreign workers are still subject to various kinds of discrimination but the discrimination is subliminal, so it causes little social unrest or friction, and the country comes in for much less criticism from the international community.

It would be difficult to completely eradicate discrimination against foreign workers, short of integrating them wholly into Japanese society in the manner of the previous scenario, but discrimination could well continue to exist without really emerging into the open. Such a scenario implies a number of prerequisites, among which two are particularly important: formal systems for immigration and employment, and some form of social segregation.

Foreign workers can enter the country in a variety of different ways. They may just want to work on a temporary basis, or they may intend to reside in Japan permanently. If clear rules and standards were laid down for each set of circumstances, there would be no reason for misunderstanding or confusion, and little unfair discrimination. If people have different qualifications and statuses regarding immigration and employment, then clearly their positions, rights, and rewards in society will also differ. They would easily be persuaded of the justice of their treatment provided their rights were spelled out in advance in the form of established rules.

Foreign workers would also have to be segregated both at work and in everyday life. If they were segregated in terms of the jobs and the type of work they did, the neighborhoods they lived in, and the ambit of their everyday activities, according to their individual propensities—their level of knowledge, skills and academic record, and social attributes—their country of origin, and the group or social class they belonged to, this would tend to minimize confusion and friction and make it less difficult for people to coexist in a peaceable manner.

If there were a clear set of rules for immigration, and people were effectively segregated socially and economically after entering the country, discrimination would be much less visible, but it would hardly cease to exist. In fact, one could say that, despite their equal formal entitlement to human rights, people would actually be subjected to the strictest *de facto* discrimination. Conditions for immigration would differ according to their qualifications and background, and there would be great differences in their working and living conditions. People would be faced with enormous barriers if they sought to break out of the occupational, residential, or social categories to which they had been confined. But to the extent that people accepted such a system of social segmentalization, problems of discrimination would not really come to the surface. Examples of this kind of sophisticated discrimination can be seen in some of the European countries which used to be colonial powers.

Toward an Open, Fair, and Self-help Nation

Which of the above scenarios, then, will Japan come to resemble most closely in the future?

On the basis of the nation's response to the foreign worker problem so far, and the somewhat passive stance of the Japanese government on the issue, it would seem that something resembling the first scenario—that of a discriminatory nation—has the highest probability of occurring.

It would probably be difficult to realize the closed-door scenario, for two reasons. First there is the sheer difficulty of totally excluding foreigners intending to work illegally. With more than three million foreigners coming into Japan each year, it would be extremely difficult in practical terms to stop people entering the country legally for such avowed purposes as tourism, and then finding illegal employment afterwards. Then there is the question of how far employers in firms and industries which have come to depend heavily on low-wage labor will be able to carry out the structural reforms—rationalization and modernization—that will enable them to survive without relying on foreign labor. Such reforms remain a critical challenge for Japan's further development as an industrialized country, and are unlikely to prove easy.

The third scenario, that of integration, will also present significant difficulties. Social integration and intermarriage will no doubt increase with the passage of time, but integration will still be relatively marginal in terms of its effect on society as a whole. However easy to imagine in theory, there is only a very remote possibility of foreign workers being absorbed into society on a large scale.

Even in immigrant nations like the United States, Canada, and Australia, where one would think conditions would favor smooth integration, there is not always perfect racial harmony, as evidenced by the various ethnic minority problems in these countries. How much more difficult, then, is social integration likely to prove in a basically single-race nation like Japan, where a mostly homogeneous people have lived in isolation, relatively far removed from contacts with the outside world for much of the nation's history?

The fourth scenario, that of refined discrimination, is close to the actual status quo in some of the west European countries like Britain and France, which ruled over large numbers of colonies in their imperial heyday. But it has not come about in countries like Japan and Germany, which had relatively little colonial experience and are burdened with the negative historical legacy of their periods of expansionism in the years leading up to World War II.

In any case, I feel this type of scenario is not worthy of serious consideration. However sophisticated the discrimination, and however stable the society may appear from the outside, no scenario that tolerates actual discrimination in society should be considered as a model for the future of Japanese society. Some nations, like Switzerland and Singapore, have laid down very strict rules on immigration and residence for foreign workers, and rigorously control their employment, but it would be difficult to adopt such methods unaltered in a country the size of Japan.[1]

In Japan, then, if the situation continues to develop as it is today, and if major efforts are not made by the government, private industry, and society, we must conclude that the first scenario, that of a clearly discriminatory nation, is the one most likely to occur. But this scenario is fraught with problems and dangers both for Japan itself and for its position in the world.

As long as the rules relating to the employment of foreign workers remain unclear and standards ill-defined, the number of illegal workers will go on increasing in line with domestic demand. Some of these people and their families will eventually remain and settle in Japan, but the absence of either the legal and institutional framework or the social infrastructure to cope with large numbers of foreign residents makes this a recipe for confusion and friction, and we are likely to end up in the extremely unfortunate position where a discriminatory class structure takes root and social prejudice becomes more widespread.

Internationally, meanwhile, this situation will tend to reinforce people's image of Japan as a closed and exclusive nation. While Japanese corporations have moved into and dominated world markets, reaping large profits in the process, the enormous employment opportunities concentrated within Japan are monopolized by Japanese nationals and remain strictly out of bounds to foreigners. Yet this official position disguises the fact that Japan is actually importing large volumes of illegal foreign labor to meet the demand from domestic industry. These illegal workers, who by some counts account for a majority of all foreigners working in Japan, have no protection under the law, are discriminated against in society, and are unfairly exploited to earn profits for Japanese industry.

Under such a scenario, this is how Japan will come to be seen by the rest of the world. And one can easily imagine the problems this will pose for Japan's future in international society. What can Japan do, then, to change direction and work toward a coexistence with the outside world that prevents such a scenario from coming about?

My own view is that Japan should make an effort to incorporate the merits of the second and third scenarios—the closed door and integration—so that it does not slide into the first, that of the discriminatory nation.

The merit of the second scenario is that it would give a strong boost to the modernization and structural reform of domestic industry and make it viable without having to depend on unskilled foreign labor. It would rationalize or convert the low-wage, labor-intensive industries and promote the modernization of low-productivity sectors. The merit of the third scenario, meanwhile, is the legal framework that would enable foreigners to live and work comfortably in society on fully equal terms with Japanese. This would create a foundation for further progress toward social integration.

To put this another way, the strong point of the second scenario is that it would create a mood of self-help by denying industry the easy option of dependence on foreign labor. As Chapter 7 explained in some detail, this would not be easy to do, but it would by no means be impossible. The third scenario, meanwhile, would create an open society in which foreigners could enjoy the same rights as Japanese. I believe, therefore, that if Japan wants to avoid the discriminatory-nation scenario, which is quite likely to occur unless positive efforts are made to avoid it, the best realistic option left to it is to try and create an "open, fair, and self-help nation."

Just a Little More Effort

While it will not be easy to achieve such a desirable outcome, steady progress could be made if all the parties concerned, each from their own standpoint, were to make just a little more effort.[2] Finally, therefore, I would like to point out some of the things that government, business, and individual people might each try to do.

The government should without delay institute a clear and systematic legal framework governing the immigration and employment of foreign workers. This might take the form of a "basic law on foreign workers."

The law should clearly stipulate the qualifications, standards, conditions and procedures required for immigration, short-term employment and long-term residence, and set out clear rules that are easily understood by anyone contemplating coming to Japan to work. As we saw in Chapter 3, the government appeared some time ago to be making an effort to do this, but regrettably seems to have reached an impasse. The priority now is enacting a basic law that is easily understood all over the world. It is said there would be numerous difficulties involved in enacting such a law because it would infringe on the interests of so many government ministries and agencies, but it is hoped that the prime minister, as the nation's political leader and supreme executive, will display understanding and leadership in ensuring that the law is passed.

As a transitional measure, the government should also institute a full-scale, practical work-and-learn program for unskilled foreign workers.

The Japan International Training Cooperation Organization (JITCO) has been advising employers on how to help unskilled trainees develop new skills. Based on the accumulated experiences of this and other organizations, a skills work-training system was formally proposed on April 5, 1993, in the form of an announcement from the Ministry of Justice. This is quite important in the sense that it opens for the first time the possibility that a yet-to-be-skilled foreign worker can engage in full-fledged work, on the condition that he or she has completed a prerequisite training program.

Now the government should do two things: make the new system known more widely around the world, particularly among those foreigners who are interested in coming to Japan to work; and establish an administrative apparatus to help employers and working trainees to acquire appropriate skills, which is the official goal of the program.

In Chapters 4 and 5 of this book I described in detail the content of the work-and-learn program I advocate as a model for such on-the-job training schemes, and it is hoped the government will make serious efforts to implement some of these suggestions.

Once the proper legal framework is in place, industry will find employing foreign workers a much smoother and more orderly business. But there are a couple of areas where special efforts are required.

Employers must adopt the principle of diversity as a premise of good management, and act in good faith to help unskilled foreign workers acquire intermediate-level skills. I have discussed the support employers can give, and its significance, so there is no need to reiterate it here.

Finally, the best thing ordinary people can do is to open their hearts and minds toward people from different cultures. While our outward appearance, country of origin, language, and customs may differ, we are all the same underneath. We all think and suffer, experience joy and sadness, and love our families just the same. Being open means being conscious of people's diversity but at the same time aware of our common humanity. The best strategy for solving the foreign worker problem is for people to strive for such fairness and openness. It is only when we have all grown into truly open individuals that "problems" such as the foreign worker problem will cease to arise.

Notes

[1] Japan Labor Research Organization, "Policy Issues Relating to the Foreign Worker Problem: A Critical Examination of Policies in the Major Nations Accepting Foreign Workers," 1991.

[2] The legal and social reaction to foreigners resident in Japan clearly demonstrates how difficult an issue it is, but by the same token indicates how important an issue it will be to the nation's future. Hiroshi Tanaka, *"Foreign Residents in Japan: Legal Barriers, Mental Gulfs"* (Iwanami Shoten, 1991).

Index